Best wishes,

Judy

NO PLACE TO BE
Voices of Homeless Children

NO PLACE TO BE

Voices of Homeless Children

Judith Berck

Foreword by Robert Coles

Houghton Mifflin Company
Boston   1992

Library of Congress Cataloging-in-Publication Data
Berck, Judith.
  No place to be: voices of homeless
children / Judith Berck ; foreword by Robert Coles.
      p.   cm.
  Includes bibliographical references.
  Summary: Details the grave situation facing homeless children and their
parents who live in shelters and welfare hotels.
  ISBN 0-395-53350-3
  1. Homeless children — United States — Juvenile literature. [1. Home-
less persons.]   I. Title.
HV4505.B47   1992   91-11432
                        CIP
                        AC
362.7′08′6942 — dc20

Printed in the United States of America
HAL 10 9 8 7 6 5 4 3 2 1

To my parents,
and to all the children and parents
I met along the way

Contents

NO PLACE TO BE
Voices of Homeless Children

Marilynne Herbert

FOREWORD
Robert Coles

In 1988 I talked with some homeless families in the greater
Boston area, and in doing so I paid special attention to the
children in those families. I have, over the years, talked
with children from a wide range of backgrounds, including
boys and girls whose parents are migrant farm workers or
tenant farmers or who live in ghetto neighborhoods and
are on welfare. Yet I have never felt so saddened and (as
a citizen) ashamed as when I talked with these homeless
young people.

I also began to realize how many of them were quite
shrewd about life — perfectly able to figure out, tersely and
concisely, the reasons for the desperate straits in which
they and their families found themselves. "We're here [in
a shelter] because they don't have enough places for us —
apartments," a girl told me. I asked her who "they" were,
and she promptly replied, "The city." In my mind I ran
through the complexities that her two-word answer evoked,
such variables as the ups and downs of the real estate
market or the high cost of property maintenance, not to
mention the effect of inflationary pressures on the cost of
living, including rent. Then I suddenly thought to myself:
this young lady of nine is quite right when she uses her
sweepingly categorical approximation. Indeed, we are all
responsible for what amounts to a moral lapse of serious

1

proportions in our civic life — that any of our families, our children, should be wandering around, unable to take for granted even the most basic of requirements, a place to sleep and find shelter, reliably and securely, day and night after day and night.

I decided to ask this youngster, Helen, for her explanation of things — how it had come about that "the city" was so inhospitable to her and her kind. Her comment was all too grimly eloquent: "It's because people look out for themselves, and they try to be nice, sometimes, but they have their own troubles (that is what the social worker said), so you can't expect too much, and that's the way it is, and it's too bad."

Indeed, "it" most certainly *is* "too bad" — a psychological disaster, at times, for countless children, and a moral disaster for the rest of us, who have yet to figure out a way, it seems, to change our nation, the world's strongest, a way that will make homelessness a thing of the past in this late part of the twentieth century. Meanwhile, children whose parents have no stable home wonder not only about their present situation but about their future condition: "I saw on television these two, they got married, and they moved into a place. They must have had jobs that paid a lot! You can't have a place if you haven't got the money they ask of you."

She was referring to the one-month security deposit, then the rent each month, not to mention money to pay for utilities and heat. Millions of us, whether we own our own homes or live in apartments, know about such costs, yet somehow we are able to meet them. Some people can't do so — thousands of parents of thousands of children in city after city across the American nation — and the result is a state of affairs that the reader will soon come to comprehend in the pages that follow: boys and girls who are, in a psychological sense, adrift, even as they wander from place to place or stay put in shelters, where they face daily trials, hurdles, and worse.

It is good that Judy Berck has done the work of making this book, a documentary effort meant to let those of us who can afford to live fairly settled lives know how it goes for those who live at the margins of society. The college and medical students I teach have sometimes asked me about the children of homeless families — wondered out loud how such a vulnerable life shapes those fated to the experience. I tell the students what I have heard and seen, but such descriptions are secondhand and inevitably lose some of the immediacy and force that a child's personal statement can have. We do need vigorous reportage on this matter — serious and compassionate and detailed journalism. But we also need witnesses who speak from their own day-to-day experience and that is what this compelling, and at times poignant, even haunting, book offers: boys and girls who tell us what they go through, list their difficulties and worries, and give expression to their hopes, their wishes, their anticipations or expectations.

What emerges, after all these children have become our teachers, have let us know about their present lives, their past disappointments, their dreams for the future, is a portrait of a segment of America — young people who have little going for them and, hence, little hope that anything is likely to go well for them in the future. This is a book about youthful vulnerability and marginality, a book about those who feel themselves to be always on the wrong side of those proverbial railroad tracks, a book that takes the measure of childhood as some among us still live it. It is, also, alas, a book that takes the measure of others: we who share this country with those children and who go about our lucky, comfortable lives while they and others like them hold on as best they can to whatever bits and pieces of this world are available to them.

In that regard, I remember a remark I heard Dorothy Day make in 1952 as she stood in one of her Catholic Worker soup kitchens, ladling out soup to a long succession of homeless people: "It is terrible for them — but terrible for us, too. They need so much right now — but I suspect plenty of us won't know how needy *we* are until we meet our Maker!" She was not thereby condemning anyone in particular, not pointing her finger self-righteously at this or that person or group of people; she was, rather, contemplating the familiar biblical paradox ("The last shall be first, and the first last") and allowing for a moment of intense and melancholy introspection, a gift to her, she knew, from those poor she was trying to feed. So this book, too, is a chance for these children to tell us about themselves and also to give us pause. What kind of world are we content to let be? Or what kind of world (with what values, lived out) might we try to establish, not only on behalf of the children we are about to hear speak, but on behalf of ourselves and our own children?

Introduction

This book is not about the many thousands of homeless adults who live in parks, huddle in doorways, or sleep on sidewalk grates. Nor is it about runaway children who live in the shadows of society. It is about children whose families have no home.

Homelessness among American families with children is an open secret. In 1990, the United Nations held a "World Summit on Children," attended by the leaders of over seventy countries. Desperate conditions for poor children around the world were spotlighted. But the illumination rarely touched on the plight of the thousands of homeless American children.

Though a decade has passed since homelessness hit America hard, homelessness among families is still on the increase today. Homeless families live in every corner of this nation, from suburban Westchester County, New York, to rural Wenatchee, Washington. They are in great cities, such as Chicago, Los Angeles, Cincinnati, St. Louis, and Washington, D.C., as well as in small towns in the backwoods. They live in shelters and welfare hotels, on the floors of relatives' apartments, in subways, in cars — wherever they can take refuge.

How does homelessness affect all these children? Terribly. It is a nightmare that leaves permanent scars. It dev-

A homeless family entering a shelter

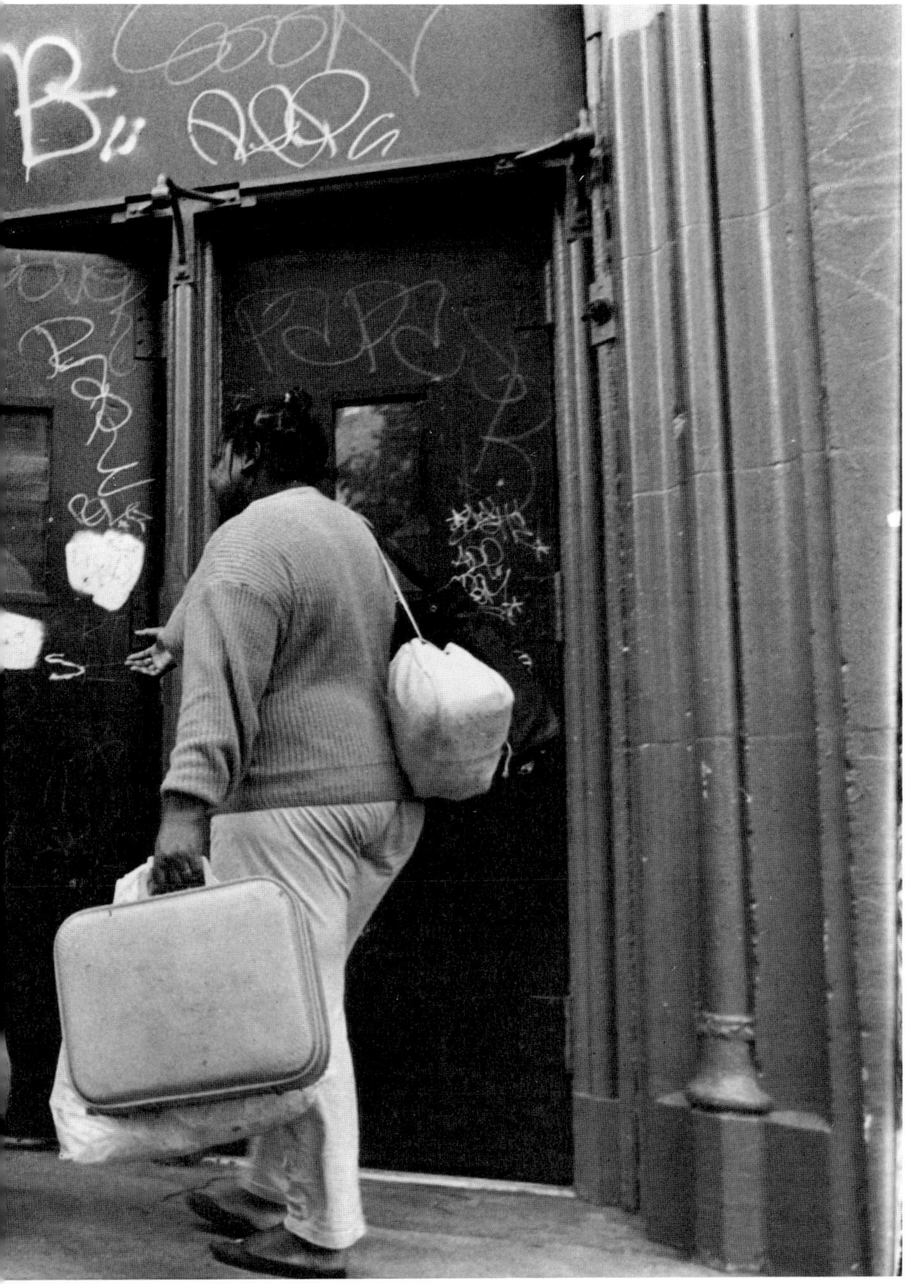

Isa Brito

astates childrens' education, health, and self-esteem. It strains family relationships. It brands children with a stigma in the eyes of their peers. Yet, these children somehow endure it, and still retain their hopes and dreams for the future. And well they should, for they *are* the future.

To find out what homelessness is really like in America, I went to the experts: the children. I interviewed more than thirty children who were living in or had recently moved from welfare hotels or shelters for homeless families in New York City. Their words are interwoven here with narrative and original poems, in an exposition of their circumstances, feelings, and opinions.

Except upon request and by explicit authorization, all names in this book have been changed.

Judith Berck
New York, 1992

Acknowledgments

Confidentiality prevents me from acknowledging by name the many articulate children I had the pleasure to meet, who shared with me from their hearts, or their parents, who trusted me in interviewing their children. They lived in the Prince George Hotel, the Times Square Hotel, the Allerton Hotel, the Bryant Hotel, the Prospect Hotel, the Madison Hotel, the Brooklyn Arms, the Hotel Martinique, the 151st Street Shelter, the East Third Street Shelter, the Catherine Street Shelter, the Lee Goodwin Residence, Rosie and Harry's Place (East Harlem Family Center), HELP I, and the Henry Street Settlement. I will never forget you, children or parents.

This book would not have been possible without the assistance of the following persons and organizations: Jack Doyle and the American Red Cross; Melvin Reeves, Director of HELP I; Daniel Kronenfeld and the Henry Street Settlement; Verona Middleton-Jeter, Director of Henry Street's Urban Family Center; Rita Zimmer and Women In Need; Mary Robinson, Director of Women In Need's Lee Goodwin Residence; Prim Greene, Director of the Association to Benefit Childrens' East Harlem Family Center; Bob Behr, Director of Camp Homeward Bound (a project of the Coalition for the Homeless of New York); Kristin Conklin, Single Parent Resource Center; and Mary Abbate, Forest Hills Community House.

I would like to thank the following people for taking the time to review drafts of this book, and for their extremely valuable comments: Steven Banks, Legal Aid Society Homeless Family Rights Project, whose tireless work has helped so many; Janice Molnar, Bank Street College of Education; Robert M. Hayes, Chairman, Coalition for the Homeless of New York; Sylvia Bost; Rose Anello; Joan McAllister, Editor of the *How . . . When . . . Where* newsletter for homeless families; and Katie Browning. The sharp insights of all the Greilsheimer kids were appreciated.

I would also like to thank the following people for their feedback on certain sections of the book: Ronald Shiffman, Executive Director, Pratt Institute Center for Community and Environmental Development, and member of the New York City Planning Commission; Terry J. Rosenberg, Director, Population Studies Unit, Community Service Society; and Dr. Irwin Redlener, Director, New York Children's Health Project.

I am greatly indebted to Barbara Fisher and The Waterways Project of Ten Penny Players, Inc., for the use of the poems written by homeless children in the project's workshops, and published in their various newsletters. I am also grateful to photographer Marilynne Herbert and to Citizens' Committee for Children of New York, Inc., for the use of her many photographs, most of which appeared in their cooperative effort, "Children of the Welfare Hotels" (Citizens' Committee for Children of New York, Inc., 1987). Thanks to Bob Behr for making available Camp Homeward Bound's newsletters and to Rita Zimmer for Women In Need's newsletters. The mural in the photo depicting "Calle de Sueños — Street of Dreams" was a project of the Creative Arts Workshops for Homeless Children, painted in 1989 on East 124th Street in Manhattan by children from a number of shelters and hotels.

I am especially grateful to Jonathan Kozol, for making this opportunity possible for me, and to Mary Lee Donovan, my patient and enthusiastic editor, who conceived the idea for this book. Additional thanks to William Greilsheimer and James Greilsheimer, for their counsel; Randy Harper; Sister Elvira; Karen Redlener; Bill Donahue; Lisa Glazer and *City Limits* magazine; Brookie Maxwell of the Creative Arts Workshops for Homeless Children; Joan Alker of the National Coalition for the Homeless; Barry Zigas of the National Low Income Housing Coalition; Clifford Krauss; and especially to Joan McAllister, for her suggestions and moral support, and to Katie Browning, who helped me survive the long haul.

List of Children's Names

Akheem, 13   Shama's brother
Angela, 11
Burton, 13   Doreen's brother
Denise, 15
Doreen, 14   Burton's sister
Douglas [age not given]
Elizabeth, 15
Jackie, 12   Jimmy and Stephanie's brother
Jenelle, 10
Jimmy, 14   Jackie and Stephanie's brother
Johnny, 12   Leon's brother
José, 12
Kareem, 14
Kwazee, 14
Leon, 14   Johnny's brother
Maria O., 11
Maria P., 18
Mary [age not given]
Melanie [age not given]
Michael, 10   Navonni's brother
Navonni, 12   Michael's sister
Newport, 17
Omar, 10
Rudy, 10

Shama, 12   Akheem's sister
Sheba, 15
Sonya, 9
Stephanie, 13   Jimmy and Jackie's sister
Tasha, 16
Tiphany, 10
Tracy, 9
Yvette, 12

"In the Homeless Hotel" by Maria P.

Homeless we are called without a place to live,
Somewhere you can call a home,
A place where we can give.
  We are not pigs,
  We're human beings with a race and creed.
  We are not animals that just mate and breed.
Once we were strong . . . But now in a way stronger.
Your pity not needed because we're poor;
Our pride supports us and helps us endure.
  Your pity not needed, but your understanding, yes.
  Being homeless is the saddest thing,
  Because some good people are suffering.
The banging on doors,
The screams in the night,
Even shootings on ground floors,
The pushers in flight.
The homeless scum is what they're called . . .
  But what about me?
  Like you, I once had hopes and dreams.
  But they're growing dim
  . . . And I'm only sixteen.

Families, with all their belongings, waiting outside a shelter placement office

1
Why? Homelessness and the Big Picture

TRACY:
When I was eight, we came here. I asked my mother where we were, and she said it's a shelter. I asked her, "What's a shelter?" and she said it's a place where homeless people are. And I asked her, "What are we doing here?" At first she didn't tell me why we were here, so I got real scared. So I asked her, "Are we homeless?" and she said yes, because the landlord hadn't been giving us enough heat and she couldn't find us another place. After that I wasn't so scared anymore, because I knew what we were here for. I said to myself, "Well, we've just got to live with it until we find a place to live."

There are homeless families in every part of this nation. Children and their parents comprise over one third of all the people in homeless shelters. It is impossible, though, to count their total numbers. One could count all the families in the shelters on a particular night, but that would tell only part of the story, leaving out the numbers of families who are turned away at the shelter doors or who stay away from the shelters out of fear. Not every state requires municipal governments to provide shelter for homeless families. In New Orleans, Louisiana, for instance, there are less than 200 shelter beds for an estimated several thousand homeless families. The rest sleep where they can — in public places, in cars, on friends' or relatives' floors. It is safe to say that there are several hundred thousand homeless families in America. Among them are perhaps half a million children.

Why are there so many homeless families in America now? Because there are more poor families who need housing than places in which they can afford to live.

Being Poor

JOSÉ:
My skateboard broke last year. I love skateboarding. My mother said I can't get a new one because she don't have the money, but she said maybe at Christmas I can have one.

One out of five American children knows the bitter taste of poverty. The numbers are even higher than that in certain parts of the country. More than forty percent of New York City's children are poor. In fact, more poor children live in New York City than there are residents of the entire state of Wyoming: an astonishing 700,000 children.

Children are poor because their families are poor. All over the country, poverty among American families has been growing. The number of poor families grew by more than thirty-five percent between 1979 and 1986 alone, years, ironically, when the economy was going strong. Today, more than one out of ten American families are poor.

Families with a single female parent are the poorest of all, a category which has drastically increased by over forty percent since 1970. A child in a family headed by a single woman, in fact, is five times more likely to be poor than a child in a two-parent household.

KWAZEE:
If you're a parent by yourself, you have to take care of everybody. It's a real burden. There's a lot of pressures. You have to save up and have a budget to make sure you get everything. Sometimes my mother couldn't get everything she needed, because she was getting us everything we needed. Like she waited five months to buy herself a new pair of shoes, because she needed to get us things. But I would do that too, because I would want my kids to look decent. Your children are a reflection of you, and you don't want them walking around looking like bums.

There are poor families of all races and creeds, but it is a fact of life in America that a child in an African-American or Hispanic family is far more likely to be poor than a child in a white family. At the start of 1990, forty-three percent of all African-American children were poor, and thirty-six percent of Hispanic children — compared to only fourteen percent of white children. The homeless family population reflects the imbalance; in most cities, nonwhites are over-represented in the shelters.

Even if a parent has a full-time job, a family can still be poor, because many jobs don't pay enough to lift a family out of poverty. A person working forty hours a week at the minimum wage, $4.25 an hour, makes only $170 a week, or $8,840 a year, which is far below the 1990 federal poverty level of $13,360 for a family of four.

JOSÉ:
My mother used to work fixing beds in a hotel. They used to pay her good — $6.00 an hour. When she finds another job, she'll have money for the rent and all that. And then my mother will get proud.

19

Poverty and scarce inexpensive housing are the root causes of family homelessness.

A "safety net" of government financial assistance programs helps families whose income falls below a certain level. Known as "welfare" or "public assistance," the programs help pay for housing, food, medical costs, and other necessities. The government pays for them from tax revenues; in this way, the public indirectly supports those who need help.

But it's just not enough these days. Decades ago, needy families could maintain themselves on welfare payments at a very modest, but decent, standard of living. Now, those on welfare must struggle for survival. For years, costs have skyrocketed, but the local welfare amounts have hardly gone up: in New York State, for instance, the Consumer Price Index rose 224 percent between 1969 and 1988, while the basic welfare grant rose by only 53 percent. Families dependent on welfare today are guaranteed to be living in poverty. In New York State, for example, a family of four on welfare has an income of only $687.70 a month, or $8,252.40 a year, far below the 1990 federal poverty level of $13,360 for a family that size. This includes a rent allotment of only $312 a month, a minuscule sum in New York's housing market.

To make matters worse, during the Reagan presidency, the federal government hacked away at the welfare programs. Since 1982, $6.8 billion has been cut from the Food Stamp program, pushing one million recipients off the program and reducing benefits for 20 million people, most of whom are children.

NEWPORT:
What really messes the family up is that you only get a little money from welfare. You need that money to go places. You need it to buy clothes. You need it to buy stuff for the baby. It's tough having no money.

Whether on welfare or working, poor families have a very difficult time finding housing they can afford. Rents have soared in recent years, forcing many poor families to pay more than half their income for rent each month. Some pay even more, sacrificing almost anything else in order to keep their homes. This means that they delve into money meant for clothing or other living expenses in order to pay the rent. But, if the time comes that a family must choose between buying food or paying the rent, they will choose food, even if the consequence is homelessness.

KWAZEE:
*We always had food. That was the main thing my
mother always got. Even if we couldn't get something
else, we'd always have food.*

The Housing Shortage

JOSÉ:
*My mother's trying real, real hard to find an apartment.
And I like that. See, if you work hard to get your
apartment, you gotta work hard to get it again if you lose
it. So we're working on it. We're trying to get it, we
almost got it.*

This country has known widespread poverty, hunger, and
unemployment several times since the Great Depression
of the 1930s. But never before has it seen poverty accompanied by family homelessness to the extent it does today. What distinguishes modern times from eras of past
hardship is a severe, persistent shortage of inexpensive
housing.

For almost two decades now, the number of places poor
families can afford to live in has been shrinking, for many
economic reasons. Thousands of buildings were abandoned
in the 1970s and early 1980s by landlords who could no
longer pay their taxes or mortgage payments because of
the rising costs of everything from heating oil to plumbers'
fees. Thousands more buildings with inexpensive apartments were destroyed by the government itself in efforts
to improve slum areas. Thousands more again were con-
verted by landlords into much more profitable condominiums or cooperatives.

In these and many other ways, inexpensive housing has
been disappearing everywhere in the nation. Between 1978

and 1987, the number of apartments that could be rented for less than $300 a month fell by 146,000 in New York City alone.

The federal government used to help cities and states greatly by giving them money to build public housing for the poor. But Washington has changed its mind in recent years — it has cut its housing budget by over 70 percent since 1978. The local effects of the cuts have been drastic. In the 1950s, 75,000 public housing apartments, known as "projects," were built in New York City. In the 1980s, only 10,900 public housing apartments were built, despite the greater need for such housing. Over 200,000 families are now on the waiting list for this housing; the wait is estimated to be eighteen years.

One effect of the housing shortage and lack of housing assistance has been a national increase in the number of families who double-up with relatives or friends. In New York alone, it is estimated that well over 100,000 poor families share apartments with other families. Though hidden from public view, these families should be counted among the homeless, for they, too, lack a stable place to live.

ELIZABETH:
The apartment we used to live in, my cousins', had a lot of people in it. There were eleven people in two rooms: me, my mother, my sisters, my uncles, my grandmother, my cousins. It was really uncomfortable. I slept in my own bed. My sisters slept on the floor with my mother, on pillows. My grandmother slept on one sofa and my aunt on the other one, and my cousin's family slept three people in one bed. With all those people it got dirty and messed up fast, so I used to clean it up a lot. We would fight all the time.

The low-income housing stock has been shrinking dramatically over the years.

MARIA P.:

The worst thing was to live with other people, because they needed their privacy as much as we did. Sometimes you need to be just with your family. A lot of times we were in the way. Sometimes I felt bad vibes — like when you know you're not wanted.

Back in 1890, a historian and photographer named Jacob A. Riis wrote about the "outrageous overcrowding" in New York City buildings where recent immigrants from Europe lived: "There were nine in the family: husband, wife, an aged grandmother, and six children; honest . . . but poor. All nine lived in two rooms, one about ten feet square that served as parlor, bedroom, and eating-room, the other a small hall-room made into a kitchen."

Riis could not have foreseen that a century later, families throughout America would be enduring conditions just as overcrowded, and just as unsuitable, because they also could not afford a decent place to live.

2

From Home to Homeless

OMAR:

I was living in the Bronx. I was seven. One day the rent was low; the next day the landlord brought it up high. We couldn't pay the rent; we couldn't afford it. We said to him, "Could you lower it down? We can't afford it." And he says, "No, you gotta pay what the rent says." I was scared. I thought they might blow up the house or something if we didn't pay the rent. So we had to leave.

How do families lose their housing in the first place? Many give it up because it has become unaffordable for them. The rent might suddenly be raised beyond their ability to pay it. Their source of income might be cut off — the family breadwinner could lose his or her job, become disabled, or die; or their welfare case might be closed, leaving no way to pay the rent.

When more affluent families run into financial straits, they might fall back on insurance, savings accounts, or, in desperation, a loan from a friend or relative. Poor families have no such resources, and typically, their extended families and friends are hardly better off themselves. For them, financial difficulty can lead to housing disaster.

NAVONNI:
We were living at my grandmother's house in Brooklyn. She decided to move to Florida, and we stayed in her house. My mother thought that she could continue to pay the rent and gas bills and stuff, but she couldn't manage on her own, because the rent was high and she didn't have that much money. So after a few months of trying to pay all the bills and still have some money left over to pay for food and clothes and everything, we had to move out.

DENISE:
My mother had worked as a nurse's aide. She was working with a patient and she slipped and hurt her back, and she couldn't work anymore. The money from her job compensation wasn't enough.

Eviction is one of the main routes to homelessness. Over 21,000 households were evicted in New York City in 1989, the vast majority for nonpayment of rent. More than a quarter of the families in New York City's shelters were evicted from their housing.

A landlord has the right to ask a court to evict a family who has not paid its rent — as long as the landlord has been giving heat, hot water, and other services to the building. Landlords depend upon the rental income to pay the costs of maintaining their buildings, and they can't do without it for long.

But some landlords pressure poor families to leave for reasons that are not legal. A landlord, for instance, may want his or her low-income tenants to move out sooner than they actually have to, so that the building can be sold, or the apartments rented out to higher-paying tenants. Some landlords are so anxious for their poorer tenants to move out that they intimidate them into leaving, or stop providing services like heat to the building. Poor tenants can't afford legal services to defend themselves against the actions of unscrupulous landlords. In eviction cases that are tried in New York's housing court, the vast majority of landlords have lawyers to defend them; most of the tenants do not.

MARIA P.:
When my father left my mother, he stopped supporting us and we had to go on welfare. After that, the landlady wouldn't take our rent check anymore. She said she didn't want it. I think it was because we were on welfare, but I don't really know the reason. But I know that after my father left, she didn't want us there anymore.

After that she started harassing us. She used to say vulgar things to the kids, and sometimes we'd act back, and call her names like "witch." Then the lady went to housing court and told my mother that she was going to have the marshal evict us. She told them we didn't pay the rent, but it was her fault because she didn't take the rent.

The night before, we started packing and we decided to sleep at my cousin's house. We took the most valuable things with us. The next morning when I went back to get the bunk beds with my uncle, the door was locked. They were inside. I could hear them breaking things that were still there. I know for a fact they're not supposed to do that. So I knocked on the door, and the landlady cursed at us and called the police. So we left.

When I saw them leave the building, I climbed in the fire escape, and with shoe polish I wrote on the wall, "Landlord Abuse," and "It's not right kicking a family

Some families leave their housing because it has become dilapidated and too dangerous.

out." Then I got the few things that were left. The bunk beds were destroyed. The couches were ripped apart and everything was broken inside. My mother was really upset.

After that we lived at my cousin's place. We moved upstairs to a little room. There was me, my mother, my brother and my sister in one little room, closet-sized, believe me!! We lived there for a while. Then that landlord wanted us out so he evicted us from there too. I guess because there were too many people in the apartment. I think that time was the worst. We came home late one day from the park, and we saw the big yellow sign "Evicted" and the marshal was there. I got upset and I started crying. We didn't know this would happen.

Some families are forced to leave their homes because their apartments or buildings have become unfit places to live. Apartments are classified as dilapidated when they are judged to be in such poor physical condition that they pose a serious threat to the health and well-being of their occupants. There are roughly 37,000 occupied dilapidated apartments in New York City. A family's living situation might become so unpleasant or dangerous that they are forced to move out. In some cases, the city itself might order a family to vacate the premises, lest the building collapse.

NAVONNI:
Where we used to live, the place wasn't in too good condition. It was a three-story building. There were a lot of holes in the building, a lot of rats. The landlord wasn't taking care of the things that had to be done. We didn't have hot water or heat from the radiators. It was freezing.

31

Fire destroys the housing of more than a tenth of the families who end up in shelters.

ANGELA:
What happened was, we were in our apartment in the Bronx, on the second floor. I have a baby brother, who was four, and a sister who was six, and I was seven. My mother was reading, and me and my sister were playing with the Nintendo. My brother was playing with his GI Joes.

All of a sudden my mother started smelling smoke. She said, "Oh my goodness." If my brother even gets a cut, my mother gets scared. Then my mother ran downstairs to her friend Laura, and they tried to go all the way downstairs, but they couldn't get through because there was fire.

My mother ran upstairs real fast, and she grabbed all three of us, me on her hip, my brother on her back, and my sister in her hands. All of a sudden a big piece of wood plopped right next to us. Then the firemen came.

My mother started reaching each of us out the window. So I went out the window, and I bounced up on one of those big white trampolines. And my sister went out the window. But then my mother said, "I'm not throwing my son out the window," cause she was afraid my brother would break his head. She said, "I'm not throwing him. If he breaks his neck, I'm gonna kill myself." So I said, "No, Mommy, just jump down with him in your hands." And she said "okay," because she listens to me. So she grabbed my brother real tight, and then she jumped, and she was so happy she started crying.

The drug trade forces many families to flee their housing.

The plagues of drugs and violence make life so dangerous in some neighborhoods that families flee.

ELIZABETH:
Where we used to live — the fourteenth floor, the top floor — was really dangerous. The roof was very close, and we used to see people up there shooting guns or fighting. One morning, somebody was dead outside. I was really scared that something would happen to my mother when she went out to work or to study somewhere. We used to be scared all the time, so my mother took us to the shelter.

Violence within a family can lead to homelessness. In all too many families, the mother, sometimes along with the children, is physically abused by her husband or boyfriend. It may get to the point where the mother flees with the children.

RUDY:

We left our apartment because my stepfather used to hit my mother and she had to get away from him. We went to stay at our friend's house. Then one day I saw my stepfather driving in a van down our block. I ran to the house and told my mother not to go out because he found us. So she didn't go out for a month, and then after that we went to the shelter.

More than half the families who eventually go to a shelter first move in with relatives or friends. Doubling-up with others might be manageable for a short time, but an apartment holding two families for long can become a very tense place to live. If the tension becomes unbearable, the guest family will move out, or be asked to leave. They may move in with other relatives or friends, until they've run out of places where they're welcome.

NAVONNI:

My aunt couldn't take it when we were staying with her. With all her kids and us it was too crowded. Between us and my aunt's family, we were ten people in two rooms. I slept on the floor. We would really argue a lot. Well, my aunt and my mother got in a disagreement. So my mother said, "Well, if that's how you feel about it, we'll just leave." So we did. That's why we came to this hotel.

Each family living in a shelter or hotel for the homeless had a traumatic experience getting there. As the following chapter will show, the trauma continues throughout their stay in the shelter system.

3

Where Do We Go Now?

JOHNNY:
You don't have any choice. You can either stay in the streets and die, or you can go in a hotel 'til you get yourself together. At least you have some place to sleep; a TV isn't that important right now. You have to think about the future; what are you going to do?

Close to five thousand families, including more than eight thousand children, live in New York City's shelter system. The largest shelter system in the nation, it encompasses seventy-eight different facilities. Families pass through it at a rate of about twelve thousand a year.

This feature of New York City's landscape is only ten years old; it came about, though, in part because of the Great Depression of the 1930s. Following the widespread destitution and hunger of that time, the idea became popular that government, rather than charity organizations, should take on the responsibility for helping those in need. This society, many Americans felt, could and should ensure that none of its citizens be forced to endure that kind of misery again.

The federal government then established national programs to help the poor, the unemployed, the elderly, and other Americans in need. Many states, too, embraced the idea that government should help those in need. In 1938, the New York State government added a provision to its constitution which declared that the "aid, care and support of the needy is a public obligation."

An unprecedented test of this resolve to help needy Americans came with the housing shortage starting in the late 1970s and early 1980s. The disturbing sight of men and women sleeping in doorways and on sidewalks, once confined to "skid row," became as common as the street signs. In New York, as in many other cities, the situation was particularly shocking. Hundreds of parents with children who had lost their housing swamped the existing shelters. Desperate families spent nights sleeping on the desks and chairs of city welfare offices, waiting for placement in a shelter. They needed help.

Outraged civic organizations and individuals brought lawsuits against the city and state governments of New York in the early 1980s. The government, they felt, was not trying to provide the "aid, care and support of the needy" mandated by the state constitution back in 1938. After bitter legal battles, the courts finally decided that men, women, and, as of 1983, families, had a right to shelter at the public's expense under this constitutional clause. The city had the obligation to provide adequate shelter to any family that needed it.

The city found itself drastically unprepared for the responsibility of aiding the homeless. Despite the fact that a housing shortage had been going on for several years, there were no plans in the event that families might need housing assistance and turn to the city for help. There was nowhere to put them all.

As an emergency measure, the city began renting rooms for homeless families in private hotels. Within a short time, dozens of hotels were being used. Commonly called "welfare hotels" because the rent is paid for by the government, they are infamous for being run-down, overcrowded, and dangerous. The city also turned several institutional buildings it owns into huge shelters, where dozens of men, women, and children sleep in cots side by side, army barracks-style, in each large room. City policymakers assumed that uncomfortable shelters would somehow deter families from becoming homeless.

Nonprofit, or charity, organizations scrambled to create more appropriate shelters, with more services to help families. These "family-style" shelters, though, have taken years to be developed, due to bureaucratic red tape, community opposition, and other obstacles. Family-style shelters are now the most common type, but there are still not nearly enough of them to replace the other kinds.

Ten years after the housing crisis became a disaster, the same shelter system is still in place in New York City, with little decline in the numbers of homeless families. And not just in New York — the welfare hotels, barracks-style shelters, and family-style shelters mentioned above can be found, in varying forms, all across the country. Later chapters discuss what life is like in each kind.

The shelters in this country are phenomenally expensive to run. Their operating expenses are paid for by the government, from the taxes paid by all Americans. The federal government pays half the shelter costs; state and local governments split the rest of the bills. In New York, the hotels charge their usual nightly room rates, which can run as high as $105 per night, or $37,800 per year, of public money — for a family of four to live in one squalid room. A lot of this money, ironically, ends up as profit in the pockets of hotel owners, despite the fact that all their "guests" are homeless. The barracks-style and family-style shelters are even more expensive than the hotels — they cost the public up to $171.17 a night for a family of four, or $62,000 yearly per family.

At a national news conference in late 1986, then-President Ronald Reagan said he heard that in New York City the government spends $37,000 a year to house a family in a run-down hotel. "Why doesn't someone build a house for that family?" he asked.

The President could have learned the answer from his own administration: federal officials themselves determined that the federal money for shelters and hotels can be used for "emergency purposes" only. The money can be used neither to rent permanent homes, nor to build them, as these uses would not fit the federal definition of "emergency." These regulations remain in effect today.

TASHA:
My aunt was tired of us living with her. My mother was scared to go to the city for help, because she'd heard about the hotels they send you to. So we went to this park. A few hours later it started getting cold out. My mother said, "Enough of this," and called the EAU.

The first stop in New York's shelter system is usually the placement office, known as the EAU (Emergency Assistance Unit). This office evaluates each family's situation, and determines which type of shelter a family can be sent to. By state law, pregnant women, newborns, and people with medical problems, are supposed to be sent only to shelters or hotels that have private rooms. Each family coming to the placement office must be interviewed by a nurse and a caseworker.

The placement and evaluation process is very slow. Families must wait for several hours before they are finally placed in a shelter. Sometimes the process gets so backed up that families are kept all night at the placement office, waiting for an opening at a shelter or hotel.

The wait for shelter placement can take many hours —
sometimes even days.

TASHA:
You have to be there after 5:00 P.M. But you might not
be out of there until four in the morning. A lot of people
are waiting for someplace to stay. People get impatient
and upset; they be tired.

JOSÉ:
They wanted to send us to a hotel in Queens, and then
they wanted to send us to another place in Brooklyn, but
they had no room. So we had to sleep on chairs all night
at the EAU.
    They don't tell you nothing. My mother thought that if
you go early, they could see you early. But they sent
people to a shelter who came to the EAU after we did.
That's not right.

From the placement office, homeless families are sent to stay in any shelter or hotel with available beds within the boundaries of New York City. The city has even used hotels in neighboring New Jersey. According to New York State law, placements to shelters and hotels are supposed to be made "in light of the community ties and educational needs of the family and the children in the family." Sadly, this law has been ignored. Most families end up disconnected by distance and circumstance from everything familiar — friends, neighbors, schools. It's as if they become lost in the middle of their own city.

JOSÉ:
It's really hard. My mother got mad because they sent us to a place really far away in Manhattan. My brothers needed to stay in their school in the Bronx so they could pass their classes. So my mother wanted us to move to a shelter up there. 'Cause in Manhattan, they had to wake up at 5:00 A.M. to get to the Bronx, and that's not good for you. But they wouldn't move us up there. It made my mother so mad, she almost used to cry. It made her really mad.

The shelters and hotels are often located in dangerous neighborhoods.

TRACY:
The bad thing about this shelter is there's a lot of drugs going around this neighborhood. I see a lot of people going around to the corner. I see they're sticking money into a window, and I see things coming back out. It's like a ghetto and I don't like to live in ghettos. I'm not trying to take it for granted, because it's better than nothing. If we didn't come here we'd probably be on the street.

41

Each shelter and hotel has a different policy regarding how long a family can stay there. Some places are willing, as long as the city is paying the bills, to keep families until they find a permanent place to live. Others agree to let families stay for only a few weeks or months. Quite a few places limit homeless families to stays of only one or two nights at a time.

The different time limits at each shelter and hotel create a nightmarish situation. Families bounce around the city like Ping-Pong balls, moving from one shelter or hotel to another, returning to the placement office each time for reassignment, until the day comes that they move into a permanent home. Parents have almost no control over where or how long their family will be living in a shelter or hotel. Children must live with the sense that there's no place where they really belong.

DENISE:
From the EAU, they put us in a shelter for one night. Then the next morning we had to leave early, at 7:00 A.M. Then we went to another EAU that night. Then they sent us to another shelter.

TASHA:
I moved at least ten times in a year and a half. I don't even remember the names of some of the hotels and shelters. Sometimes the hotel would keep you for only two weeks and then you would have to go somewhere else.

SHAMA:
The worst thing was being in the hotel, and being told we were going to move, but not knowing how soon. I was like, "Oh, my God! Yes!! I'm moving!" I couldn't

*believe it. I was so glad I was moving out of that place.
So happy. But we had to wait and wait and wait so long
I wish I wasn't told. I was so impatient. Finally we
moved after two months. We were so glad, but now we
have to move again.*

MARIA O.:
*At the last shelter, the fifth place we were at last year,
we had fun. There were a lot of people there who cared,
and they liked you, and my mother had a lot of friends,
and I had my best friend Elizabeth, and I had fun with
her. Then we had to split apart when I moved. I started
crying, because I didn't want to leave.*

Shelters and hotels do not have the room or security for
families to bring all their possessions along with them.
Whatever possessions a family might have tend to get lost,
stolen, or scattered.

MICHAEL:
*My mother packed away my radio and my walkie-talkie.
I hope she didn't leave the batteries in it. I'm scared
because if you leave the batteries in there they can mess
up the radio. She packed all our stuff in boxes and put
them in her friend's house.*

All too often, homelessness undermines family unity.
Many parents try to spare at least one of their children the
trauma of the shelter system by sending a child (usually
the eldest) to stay with relatives or friends, or even in foster
care, until the family can be reunited in a permanent home.

JIMMY:
*I was ten. My mother had this apartment and they didn't
give her no heat. It was in the wintertime, and she didn't*

43

want us to get sick or nothing, so she placed some of us in foster homes.

I remember she sat everybody down in the room and told us what had to be done. She wanted us to have heat and hot water and a place to rest our heads and stuff like that. She was going to go out and find a place for us to live, but she couldn't take all the kids with her to look for an apartment.

At first I didn't want to go. But she said, "No, it will be good for you." Nobody liked it, but we had to do what she said anyway, 'cause she's our mother. I was angry. Then I said to myself, Well, she's doing what's best for us — she wouldn't try to hurt us.

It was hell. You don't know nobody — you have to stay with people if you like them or not. In the beginning it broke us apart — we all missed each other and stuff. Every two or three weeks they had a visitors' day. All of us would come together at this place, like a family reunion. It was happy, sad, everybody wanted to go home.

It took my mother a while to get us back from foster care, almost a year. It was fun when we got back together, being with everybody you know, people who love you and stuff like that.

Homelessness is often a long-term situation. Families typically are homeless for up to a year.

Where do families go when they leave the shelter system? The city does provide a small number of permanent apartments to homeless families who have lived in the shelter system for nine months or more. Housing experts emphatically point out, however, that these apartments amount to just a drop in the bucket compared to the tremendous need for them.

44

Part of the reason so few apartments are made available to those who need them most lies in the attitude of city officials toward the problem. If they provide a lot of apartments to families in the shelter system, city officials fear that other families who don't really need them will "become" homeless in order to get one of these apartments. Advocates for the homeless insist that this attitude is cruel and illogical: families become homeless because they have no choice.

Those families who do receive an apartment through the city are not in for a luxurious experience. According to housing experts, many of these apartments are in crumbling, dilapidated buildings. These buildings tend to be located in the city's most crime-ridden, barren neighborhoods, least equipped with social services and municipal resources to help homeless families get back on their feet.

Most homeless families eventually leave the shelter system on their own. If they are lucky, they settle in decent, stable housing and are able to get on with their lives. But many move into situations no better than those they left in the first place. Some families are so desperate to leave the shelters that they settle for disastrously bad housing. Others simply double-up once again with relatives or friends, or return to an abusive situation.

Whether a family ultimately prospers depends on many factors, including the stability of their new situation, the strength of the family itself, the quality of the housing, the resources in the new neighborhood, and the ability to establish a supportive network in the community. It is a sad fact that more than a third of the families seeking shelter are coming back for the second, or even the third time. The shelter system, therefore, can be home for a very long time in the life of a child.

4

When Home Is Hell: Living in a Welfare Hotel

SHAMA:

I didn't even know what a hotel was. I thought it would be clean, rooms with white sheets and little hotel soaps, and the beds made a certain way, everything in order, and people cleaning the rooms, like a hotel! That's what I thought it would be like. It's different. My mother told us, but she couldn't explain, she probably didn't know what to expect either.

Hundreds of homeless families endure punishing conditions in welfare hotels. When picturing these hotels, you must forget the standard image of a hotel. In New York City, as in many other cities and towns across the country, the hotels that shelter homeless families are far from luxurious. Some, to be sure, were once places of elegance and still boast ballrooms with chandeliers and gilded ceilings. These hotels are now best known for overcrowded, sordid living conditions — and danger. In them, entire families are squeezed into one or two tiny, squalid rooms.

SHAMA:

The first time we went to our room, I was so scared to go in. I said, "Oh, my God!" I was holding on to my mother — we just followed her around. There were

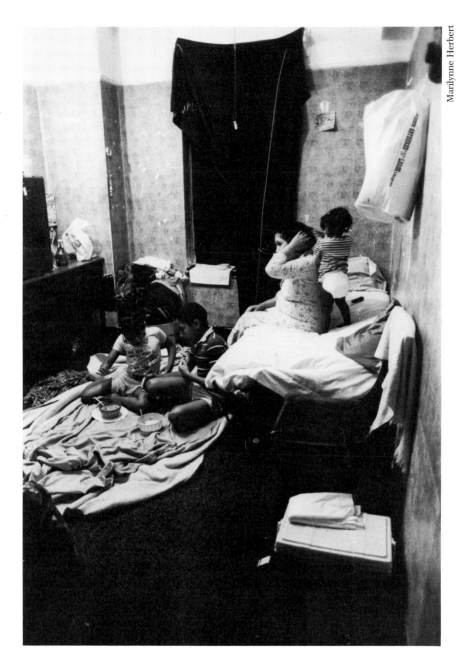

A family in their one room in a welfare hotel — there are not enough beds, and no table.

mattresses on the beds with mice feces on them. No sheets or anything. It was late, like 12 o'clock, and we just stayed on the beds, because we couldn't go anywhere. It was so tiny and yucky. It was so dirty. You wouldn't want to be there.

JIMMY:
The worst thing about the hotel was no space. I have four brothers and three sisters. We were all in two tiny rooms. It was so aggravating. All the boys were in one room and the girls in the other, with a door in between. We had bunk beds — they took up all the space. There wasn't any room even for a table. We lived like that for two years.

AKHEEM:
There were only two beds in the room for the three of us. My sister slept in my bed. She got on my nerves, because she would wake me up at night when she was scared. Then she would get up and sleep in my mother's bed.

SHAMA:
Imagine yourself stuck with two other family members in one room. I would feel trapped being there; there was no place to breathe, for the kids to play around. You need space for your things. My mother put shelves up, but things were falling down all stacked up like that. We were constantly looking through our trunks. You wouldn't want your friends to come over and see all that. They would probably make fun of you or something.

"Mixed Feelings of Being Homeless" by Vivian

Being homeless
makes me sad,
and living in this small pad
drives me mad.
   And sometimes I feel like a freak
   not able to seek
   happiness,
   until I'm out of here
   and lose some of the fear.
But for now this is my home
which I could never bring myself to call
my own.

The hotels' basic facilities often don't work. Health and safety problems, such as corroded and leaking plumbing, sporadic heat and hot water, broken elevators and faulty electrical wiring, are common. Some hotels have peeling lead paint on their walls, with lead in concentrations ten times higher than the law permits. Lead is a poison that causes brain damage. The lead contained in paint chips poses a danger to young children, who tend to put everything they can reach in their mouths.

SONYA:
I really hated our room at the Brooklyn Arms, because the ceiling in the bathroom fell in. That's why they moved us down to the fifth floor. And on the fifth floor, it was still no better, because there was a leaky pipe in the bathroom which made a big puddle of water, and most of the lights didn't work.
   We used to live on the fifteenth floor. The elevators were never working. We had to walk all the way up and

49

all the way down, even the mothers with their strollers.
That's what I hated. When I had to walk all the way up
by myself it was scary.

The people who own and manage some of these hotels
have been cited by city agencies for neglecting the cleaning, garbage pickup, and extermination. With a constant,
automatic supply of homeless residents provided and paid
for by the city, the hotel management can get away with
letting things slide.

STEPHANIE:
The mice would come out in the daytime sometimes.
You couldn't even leave bread on the top of the
refrigerator because they would get up there. We tried to
block the mouseholes, but the mice kept opening them
back up.

DOREEN:
We stayed one night in a hotel in the Bronx, the
Prospect. It was awful. There was a hole in the wall big
enough for a person to walk through. There was blood
on the sheets, and bugs on the soap. All we could do was
throw a blanket over the top of the wall to cover the hole,
and we slept there because it was too late to go
somewhere else.

SHAMA:
We lived on the first floor, facing the courtyard. When
you looked outside the window, everything was all dirty
with garbage. Flies kept coming in from the courtyard
and rats too. We had to keep the window closed all the
time. So it got really hot in there. The summer was really
hot.

Only some hotel rooms have private bathrooms inside them. Otherwise, families share public bathrooms in the hallway.

SHAMA:
We had a bathroom on our side of the hall, but the toilet didn't work, and the shower didn't work. So we had to look all over the hotel for a working bathroom we could use. We lived on the first floor and there were four floors. Sometimes we had to go up to the fourth floor to look for a working bathroom.

Most hotels have no kitchens in the rooms, and serve no meals. Families receive a "restaurant" allowance of no more than $3.33 per person per day, or $1.11 a meal, which at New York prices doesn't buy much to eat even at a "fast food" restaurant. To stretch their food allowance, many families buy groceries and cook on "hot plates" — small electric burners that plug into the wall. Unless they have such a heating source, there is no way for them to sterilize bottles for babies or to eat hot meals.

JIMMY:
We had to cook on two irons of the hot plate, which took forever. It took hours to heat up two big pots and cook enough food for everybody. Before they gave us a fridge, we had to stick food out the window, especially the milk for the babies, so it would be cool.

AKHEEM:
We had to cook all our own meals because we're vegetarians. When the inspectors came by we had to hide the hot plate under the bed. Families need to be able to cook without sneaking in stuff. It's not right to feel like you have to hide when you're cooking.

Children playing outside a welfare hotel (now closed)

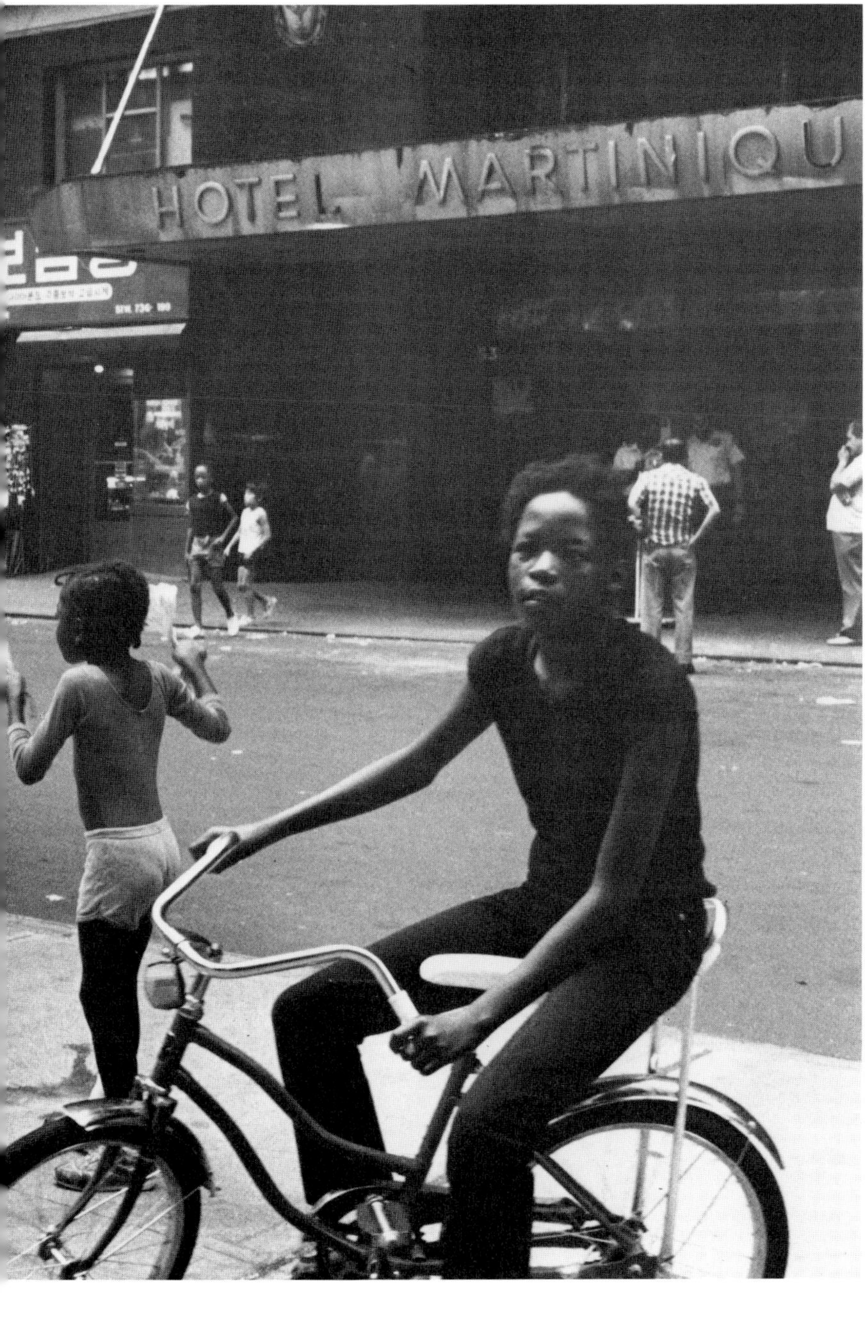

Marilynne Herbert

JIMMY:
Since we had no kitchen sink, we had to wash dishes in the bathtub. We had to sit on the floor or sit on the bed to eat, because we had no table or chairs.

When we first moved out, my younger brothers and sisters, they'd never even seen a kitchen table before — because they were born in the hotel, or were babies, and we lived there for two and a half years. One of them didn't even sit at the table — he sat on the floor like we had to at the hotel. He'd never seen it any other way. My six-year-old sister, instead of washing dishes in the sink, she washed them in the tub, because she was so used to that.

Many of the hotels are in neighborhoods that the average person would think twice about visiting with children, such as New York City's Times Square, infamous for its pornography, drug trade, prostitution, and crime. Neighborhood drug dealers ply their trade outside and inside the hotels. Children within the hotels find themselves face to face with drugs and danger.

MARY:
Really, you couldn't feel safe . . . because when you stepped out your door [into the hotel hallway] you had the guys selling drugs. The police would bang on your door with the guns in their hands and you would open the door and there was a gun in your face and you'd be so scared you couldn't talk. The police came around all the time because of the drug selling. They were looking for one of the drug dealers who killed someone or shot someone . . . All the time. It was like an everyday thing. You couldn't walk down 42nd Street because of all the drug dealers.

SHAMA:

When we moved in, we found crack vials everywhere.
We even found one with crack inside of it. And that's
dangerous because, what if a little kid didn't know
better? He could have eaten it. I didn't know what that
was either, because I wasn't around any of that before.
I didn't know what those drugs looked like.

People down the hall would cook the crack, boil it. You
could smell it. And it stunk. It made you feel sick to your
stomach. I felt like throwing up. It got so bad.

One time I went up to the fourth floor to use the
bathroom. I was so scared when I went up there,
because I saw this lady smoking reefer or something.
She looked very mean. And she was looking at me. I
pushed the elevator button and it wouldn't go. I was
afraid to go down the stairs because she was blocking
them. She was standing right there looking at me. I
finally said, "Excuse me" and pushed by. I just ran really
fast down the stairs to get away from the lady with the
reefer.

Along with the drug trade comes violence and crime.

YVETTE:

My mother is afraid to let me go downstairs. Only this
Saturday the security guard at the hotel was killed on my
floor . . . People are afraid to open the door to even look
out. I once found needles and other things that drugs
come in, in the hallway.

Our apartment was broken into when we were out.
They stole our radio and alarm clock. We have a TV but
they didn't get that because we hide it in the closet
under other things every time we leave the rooms.

NAVONNI:
One night we were sleeping, and someone pushed our door open, and my mother said, "Who's there?" And he ran away. We were all too scared to get up and close the door. He could have come back the same night. But that night, God was with my mother and told her to wake up. It was so scary.

DOREEN:
One thing the dealers would come in the hotel for, which was really dangerous, was to hide out. Sometimes they'd get on the bad side of certain people by stealing their crack or something, and then those people would come to the hotel looking for them. And they had guns. So it was really dangerous for that person to be on your hall.

One time these dealers were mad at someone, and one day they just machine-gunned the section of the block where our hotel was. They could have hit anybody. Some people came into the hotel looking for this guy once. They came in with knives into the hallway and they stabbed him, in front of me and my brother. That was awful.

MARIA P.:
People would shoot out the window and we didn't know if it was coming our way, so we would duck and hide on the floor. It was like Vietnam.

Some families are put up in hotels where, it is well known, prostitutes bring their clients.

LEON:

*The worst place was this one hotel where they were
renting rooms on the first floor to whores. Sometimes we
would be standing at the front of the hotel, and this lady
would come up to ask you, "Wanna go in a room?" To
anybody.*

The very people who are supposed to protect homeless
families are sometimes part of the problem.

DOREEN:

*I felt like I was never safe. Nobody was. Really. It was
the management's fault people were getting in. If you
wanted to do drugs upstairs and you didn't want anybody
bothering you, you gave the security guard five dollars.
You could go upstairs and no one would know. Dealers
would come in to count their crack or store their goods,
or whatever it was they needed at the time.*

SHAMA:

*I remember that a security guard kept asking me these
weird questions. I didn't know if he was teasing me or
not. He kept asking me, "Where can I buy happiness?"
He was serious, too. He kept on asking me. He would
say, "I want a bag, I want a pound. I want the white
kind. What color do you have?" I was like, "What is he
talking about?" He went on and on.*

In some welfare hotels, especially the larger and more
drug-ridden ones, the atmosphere can be so threatening
that children and parents feel afraid all the time.

MARIA P.:

When I first got there I wanted to leave. There was a lot

Most hotels have no kitchens. Many families cook with illegal hot plates.

of screaming and fighting. I was afraid of getting robbed — I was afraid of everything. It was like a little city of its own. All the vandalism was there, the mugging, raping, drugs, everything was there.

SHAMA:
I was really scared of the people there. I didn't want to stay there by myself. My mother didn't want to leave us there. So she'd tell us to go to the library. She didn't leave us in the hotel alone. I was even scared when I was asleep. I had a lot of nightmares that would wake me up.

New York City officials admit that many of the welfare hotels are not appropriate places for children to live. They insist, though, that they have no choice but to use them.

City caseworkers in the hotels do try to help families find and move into permanent housing, make arrangements for school, and put their lives in order. Volunteer groups serve meals and run programs at some hotels. The help available, though, is hardly enough to meet the needs of so many families; nor can it make welfare hotels less miserable places to be.

"Family In Need" by Bill

Homeless people
Are people with blues.
Living their problems
In one little room.
   Children live
   In darkness and with secrets
   When wanting to talk,
   Sometimes they're speechless.
Parents are trying
For a better way
While some are distracted
And here to stay.
   Giving up hope and
   Stopping their trying,
   More people are homeless
   More children are crying

5

Human Warehouses: Living in a Barracks-Style Shelter

MARIA P.:

When we got to the shelter, that's when I really cried. Me and my brother were crying because we never wanted to go to a place like that. I never thought it would come down to that for us, a good family. For something like that to happen to us was shocking, and it changed us all. I remember a guard said to me, "Don't worry, it's not that bad. You see everybody is sleeping and quiet." But I kept crying. I was eating my sandwich and crying.

Shelters in which many people sleep in the same room are called "barracks-style" because they resemble army barracks. Rows and rows of beds are lined up in very large rooms, each with up to one hundred beds. These buildings were not originally designed to shelter families. Schools, office buildings, a hospital, and a gymnasium have been used as shelters in New York City.

Barracks-style shelters, operated by city workers, are intended to provide the bare necessities that people need to survive: beds, meals, and bathrooms; certain basic items, such as soap, toothpaste, diapers, milk, and juice, are supplied by shelter staff. Staff members also provide minimal health care, help in finding schools for children, and other very limited services.

60

To families who possess almost nothing and have no-where else to go, a place that supplies these basics is a blessing. On the other hand, living in an institution has terrible drawbacks. Privacy, not strictly necessary for survival, is completely sacrificed. Men, women, teenagers, young children, and babies — all strangers — sleep in view of each other in the large, open rooms. There is no escaping the noise other people make at night — talking, snoring, babies crying.

Individual family boundaries cease to exist. Parents cannot stop their children from witnessing whatever behavior people around them choose to exhibit. It can feel very strange living in the same room with strangers, especially for fearful children, and women uncomfortable with men they don't know.

ANGELA:
Imagine a real big, big area, with a lot of families. Oh my goodness, I can't count how many beds are in each room. Our four beds are pushed up together, and then the next family's beds are pushed up together. We've slept like that for five months.

JOSÉ:
The shelter is something really really bad. Each family has its beds and a locker. Everybody can see each other.

At 11:00 P.M. they turn off the lights, so everybody's supposed to go to sleep. If you have to get up and go to the bathroom, you have to walk through all the beds in the dark without bumping anybody. People talk when you're trying to sleep. Sometimes people argue, and I get scared because I think it's about my family. So I get up to check that my brothers are okay. Then I can sleep again.

There are some new families who get to the shelter

61

*late at night. The guards turn on the lights so they can
get to their beds, and then people get angry. Sometimes
I miss breakfast because I can't sleep, and then I can't
wake up in time.*

NEWPORT:
*There are always some eyes looking at you. You might
think nobody is looking at you, but they're looking. It
makes you kind of paranoid. Everybody's watching you
put your socks on.*

ANGELA:
*A year ago, people had to block you if you wanted to
change your clothes. Now there are some white plastic
partitions you can change behind.*

Like the sleeping rooms, the bathrooms are large and
institutional, with rows of sinks, showers, and toilets. People must carry out their most private activities in the constant company of strangers. With so much use, the facilities
often break down, and are almost impossible to keep clean.

MARIA P.:
*The ladies' bathrooms are disgusting and dirty. It's really
nasty. You have to wait to get in because everybody
changes their clothes in there. There are no curtains and
everybody can look at you use it.*

MICHAEL:
*There isn't a boys' and girls' bathroom at this shelter.
They used to have them — one door used to say "boys,"
the other door used to say "girls." Now everybody uses
the same bathrooms.*

In this group setting, individual comfort or convenience

In barracks-style shelters, families have no privacy.

becomes a luxury. There are hardly any chairs or tables, and few indications that the shelters are home for hundreds of children.

JOSÉ:
They give you this camp bed, this cot, it's really hard. My back hurts a lot sometimes. My mother gets angry about that, because she doesn't want us to sleep on a bed that can give you a pain in your back.

There are some electrical outlets but they're all plugged up. So you can't use your alarm clock unless it has batteries. To iron your clothes, you have to take turns, because they only let you use the one outlet on the second floor. You have to wait until everybody else has ironed all their clothes.

Nobody can plug in their TV, so there's only one big TV for everybody. We can only see TV when they allow it. You have to go early to get a seat, because there's hardly any chairs. This one mean lady, she thinks she's the boss. We have to watch what she wants and be quiet or she gets us kicked out. So every time she leaves, we change the channel. When she comes back, she yells at us.

There's one water fountain on each floor, and one pay telephone. There's a laundry, but you have to sign up for it the night before. They only have a couple washers and dryers for everybody, and they break a lot. People get in big fights over doing the laundry.

These shelters, like most welfare hotels, have no kitchens. Families eat in one large cafeteria, where three meals a day are served. Parents must feed their babies and toddlers amidst chaos, noise, and confusion, and see to it that older children, and they themselves, get enough to eat. Without kitchens to cook in, parents can't be sure about what their children are eating.

NEWPORT:
A shelter is a bunch of people in a room, and a cafeteria. They serve this junk food, cooked up on a piece of plastic, slapped together, and they give it to you. They don't give you seconds.

I wouldn't eat dinner at all; I would wait until the morning. The best meal was breakfast. But I got tired of that every day: sausage all dried up, pancakes that tasted like flour. The syrup tasted like jelly or something, and the milk was sour all the time. One time I opened the

64

milk and there were chunks in it. I couldn't drink it at all. I threw it on the floor and got in trouble for that. I lost a lot of weight. My uncle and aunt would come by and give us food. I don't know what we would have done without them — we would have had to eat that nasty food.

JOSÉ:
My mother worries that my brother will get sick because he doesn't eat the shelter food — it makes him throw up. So she has to spend money for his food, and we hardly have any money to begin with.

With so many people crowded into a few rooms, it's difficult for shelter managers to keep everybody safe and things running smoothly. To help control the environment and maintain order, guards are posted inside the shelters, even in the sleeping areas. For those who must live with it, the constant gaze of guards compounds the feeling of being constantly on display.

NEWPORT:
There's a lot of freaky guards. They are always watching you — it makes you feel like you're doing something wrong. Everything in the shelter is negative.

MARIA P.:
Most of the guards are men, even though most of the parents are mothers. Some of them would look at you like they wanted you. I really hated that.

In a private apartment, doors and walls protect people from dangers outside. In the large, open spaces of a barracks-style shelter, children and parents are much more vulnerable. Posting metal detectors and guards at the shelter entrances are ways these shelters try to make up for the lack of personal protection. These measures intensify the sense for children that they themselves are being scrutinized.

MARIA O.:
When you come in or out, they have these metal detectors. Every time it beeps, they search you. Once it went "beep" on me. I said, "Am I supposed to take off my clothes?" And they said, "No, don't take off your clothes." I didn't get searched because I'm a little girl, and it only made a beep because it wasn't working.

As a precaution, people not staying at the shelters are strictly forbidden, except in confined visitor's areas. This poses a problem for parents who have young children, since not even a relative or friend is allowed to come into the shelter to babysit. Strict rules prohibit parents from going out and leaving children under twelve in the shelter, even if another parent in the shelter is willing to supervise the children. There are no daycare facilities in these shelters, which means that parents can't leave the shelter to look for an apartment or a job, or even go to the corner store, without taking their children along. Their movement is restricted, impairing their ability to better their situation.

TASHA:
It's really crazy. If you got seven kids, and one gets sick, all your kids got to go with you to the hospital. You can't leave them there with somebody.

All the shelters have caseworkers who are supposed to explain shelter rules, evaluate each family's needs, make referrals to local social service organizations, and meet with families every two weeks, to see what progress they have made in finding what they need. But just as in the welfare hotels, the caseworkers each have dozens of families to help, and very little time for each one. Families typically meet with a caseworker only once during their stay.

Families don't know how long the barracks-style shelter will be their home. Many others may come and go before it is their turn to leave. And even then, a home of their own will not be the next stop. The vast majority of families are simply shuttled somewhere else within the shelter system.

6

Family-Style Shelters

SHAMA:

I felt really happy when we moved here; I was really glad. It's big — it's amazing. There's room and everything. My bedroom now is bigger than the room that the three of us were in in the hotel, and I appreciate that. It's not permanent, but I still appreciate it.

JOHNNY:

At the hotel, sometimes the kids would come home from school with their friends, and they'd be embarrassed to go in. But they didn't make this shelter look like a hotel from the outside. It's one of the best buildings on the block.

On the whole, family-style shelters are the most tailored to the needs of children and parents. Unlike welfare hotels, which are operated as businesses, family-style shelters are owned and operated by charity (nonprofit) organizations founded to serve the needy, or by the city. The American Red Cross is perhaps the most familiar of the nonprofit groups. Known best for providing relief to hurricane and earthquake victims, the American Red Cross also operates several family-style shelters in New York City and elsewhere.

Those who set out to design a family-style shelter face fundamental and difficult questions. Should each family's living area be exactly like a regular apartment, with separate bedrooms for parents and children, a bathroom, and a kitchen? Or should each family share facilities with others? How much privacy and space does each family really need? What staff and services would be best for them? Are the plans realistic in light of how much money there is to spend on them? There are no right answers to these questions. The philosophy of the designers, the amount of money available for the project, and state shelter requirements shape the final outcome of each one.

Some of the planners of the family-style shelters in use today decided that homeless families need the privacy, space, and facilities of a typical apartment as much as any other family does. The better the living environment, the easier time families would have stabilizing their lives, the planners believed. They designed shelters so similar to standard apartment buildings that the shelters could be turned into permanent housing, if the day comes when shelters are no longer needed.

Other shelter planners decided it would make more sense for each family to have only one room, and share a kitchen and bathroom with other families. Private apartments, they reasoned, are not necessary, since presumably families would be there for only a short time; nor are private apartments cost-effective — a building can hold more families if each one has less space. This design often results in families living in one crowded room for a long period of time.

MARIA O.:
My mother has a room, my brother has a room, my two sisters have a room. We have a kitchen. I share a bedroom with my other sister. It's a real apartment.

69

At some shelters, families stay in decent, private apartments. Shelters, though, can't replace a home.

ELIZABETH:
Our apartment at the shelter has only one room, but me and my sister have beds. And there's another bed for my mother.

A place to stay is all some families need in order to pick themselves up by their bootstraps. There are other families, though, who have problems apart from their lack of housing. Parents may have dropped out of school, for instance, experienced domestic violence, unemployment, or drug abuse. Some homeless families need a lot of help to return to independent living. To be sure, homeless families experience these circumstances in no greater proportion than other poor families. The lack of stable housing, however,

70

compounds any other problems a family might have.

Family-style shelters address these problems by providing social services. Recreation, an on-site nurse, and individual casework are required by state law. The caseworkers meet with each family and devise a plan to help them restore control over their lives, deal with ongoing problems, and return to independent living. Shelters are supposed to help families find the services they need, such as job training, and medical, mental health, or child-care services. If shelters themselves don't provide a service, workers are supposed to refer families to organizations in the neighborhood. Unfortunately, neighborhood services are terribly scarce, especially in the poor areas where the shelters tend to be. The more services available on the shelter premises, the greater the chances that families will get the help they need.

JOHNNY:
They have daycare at the shelter so the parents can get out and try to find an apartment, or get a job until they have the right amount of money to get a house. While that's happening, they don't have to worry about the little kids.

In their efforts to help families, many of these shelters provide even more services than they are required to. Some offer workshops in job hunting and employment skills. One shelter runs a mail presort business on the premises, where homeless parents make money and gain work experience by sorting, sealing, and bagging sacks of mail for companies throughout the city. The money earned goes into a bank account for use once permanent housing is found. Some shelters offer informational classes on nutrition, AIDS, the importance of immunizing children against disease, and other health topics. Others have workshops for young or inexperienced parents to improve their ability to cope with raising a family.

Many shelters provide individual and group counseling for parents and children. A few have programs to help people who are addicted to alcohol or other drugs free themselves from their habit and put their lives back together.

KWAZEE:
They have certain age groups come down to the community room and talk. Right now we're having a group where teenagers sit around and talk to the counselor about our problems. Like sometimes we discuss why we became homeless, and how it makes us feel. Sometimes we just talk about things that are happening in the world.

Caseworkers and counselors must help families without encouraging them to become dependent upon the shelter — once a family moves into a permanent home, it must be able to fend for itself. One crucial goal of a shelter, therefore, is to help families help themselves.

ELIZABETH:
When we first came to the shelter, we were on welfare. They helped my mother start studying again to finish college, and to keep on studying so she could graduate and find a place to work at. Now she's in a good job working with handicapped kids, and kids that can't talk. She's not on welfare anymore, and she's doing things on her own. She really worked hard to finish what she was doing. I think her life is happier. Things are getting easier and better. I'm proud of my mother.

72

One of the most important services that shelters provide is helping families find permanent homes. Counselors connect parents with housing programs that have vacancies, help them get on waiting lists for apartments, fill out applications, or make appointments for interviews with landlords. In some shelters, formerly homeless parents are brought in to talk about what to expect when setting up a new home. It is no wonder that families in this kind of shelter typically move to their own homes twice as fast as those living in welfare hotels.

Family-style shelters feel different than welfare hotels and barracks-style shelters.

KWAZEE:
Everyone there looks out for each other and comes around and asks you if you're okay. It's like a big family. We lend each other everything — food, clothes, money, or whatever. At the hotel you couldn't do that because everyone had this big chip on their shoulder, and was too scared of everything.

ELIZABETH:
This place is a good place, because they give people everything they need in here and they have safety for their children and themselves. They give you your own apartment where you can live on your own with your children. It's better than the other places, where people have to live all together and it's very dangerous.

Still, living in a family-style shelter is hardly a typical family experience. Normally, parents determine the rules and guidelines for their children to follow, as well as the rewards and punishments. In shelters, children must live by rules not made by their parents. For example, shelters may dictate where, when, and how young children can

73

play, or how late teenagers can stay out. And parents must abide by bureaucratic rules not necessarily in the best interests of their family. Some shelters forbid overnight guests, for instance, even if the guest is an unmarried father who wants to spend time with his children, or an aunt trying to bolster a mother's spirits. In some shelters, residents are closely monitored by staff at all times, to ensure that the rules are followed.

JENELLE:
At 9:00 P.M., all your company has to leave. At 11:00 P.M. people who live on the inside can't go outside again. At midnight, the people inside can't visit another apartment inside. They have people on each floor to monitor everything. They're always checking up on what you're doing.

TRACY:
My mother just wants to get us out of here. She doesn't want it always being so restricted around here because of the rules. It's very hard to live like that.

"Homeless Saratoga" by Mike

Living in here is really hard.
There's gates all around
and the windows got bars.
To leave the building
you have to sign
and you got to come in
at a certain time.
If you do something wrong
you will get kicked out.
That's what this place
is all about.

Other shelters find that they don't need a whole lot of rules or monitoring.

DENISE:
At Henry Street, it's just like a regular apartment. You get your own key. My mother can cook, and we can have people visit; she can have her sisters over to gossip. They don't tell you when to go to bed, or when to turn off the lights.

MARIA O.:
Anybody can sleep over your house. When we moved from the hotel to this shelter, I was so happy I wanted all my friends to sleep over my house.

All shelter planners must decide what and how many rules are necessary, as well as what to do when parents or children break the rules. Should any family that breaks even the slightest rule be forced to leave? Where else would they go?

Whether a shelter is rigid or relaxed, spartan or comfortable, intrusively run or private, one thing is true of all of them: no shelter can take the place of a real home.

KWAZEE:
The worst thing is that you don't have a place you can call home, because it belongs to someone else. After you leave someone else will move in. People in the shelter try to make you feel at home. But you can't call it your place, it's not really yours.

7

School on the Fly: Getting an Education

NAVONNI:
One time, I had a hundred-page book I had to read for school, and I read it in one day. I started around seven or eight o'clock, and I finished around ten or eleven. I was so amazed because I don't like to read books that much. But that book, I read it, and I had it in my hand every step that I took. I could just picture the whole thing in my mind.

KAREEM:
I'm great at math, but history, that's something I can't do — I can't memorize. I just give up on dates. I can remember people but not dates.

Children of homeless families, like all children, vary in how much they like school, as well as in their aptitude for it. Some love school, others hate it. Some are academically gifted; others are terrible students. Most fall somewhere in between. Unlike other children, though, homeless students face enormous obstacles to getting an education.

According to New York State law, all children under the age of sixteen *must* go to school, whether or not they have a permanent home. But as discussed in Chapter 3, families are placed in shelters or hotels anywhere within New York

City's five boroughs. Children often end up far from the school they had been attending.

Consequently, some homeless children travel long distances by public transportation, just so they can stay in a school they know.

KWAZEE:
My aunt said I should stay in one school because some schools teach you different things or in a different way, and it gets confusing. And moving around, they might mess up your records or lose them. I'd rather stay in one school where it's stable and everything. When you move to another school, you have to make new friends and stuff. So if you stay in one school you're comfortable and you know where your friends are at.

It's easier for older children to keep going to the same school, because they are able to travel by themselves using public transportation. But children too young to travel alone must be accompanied.

JIMMY:
I had to get up around five in the morning. I would leave the hotel around six to take my younger brother and sister to their school in Brooklyn. Then I would come back to Manhattan to my school. My older sister or my mother would pick them up in the afternoon. I would get to school late pretty often.

JACKIE:
We had to escort the little ones to the classroom. Our mother had to show us the way so we would remember.

A student trying to do homework in a hotel room

Even if a child does not switch schools, a life of bouncing from shelter to shelter is bound to hurt his or her education. Each time children move, they miss an average of five days of school.

KAREEM:
Even though I've lived in a lot of places in the last three years, I did go to the same school. But every time I moved I had trouble. I would have to miss at least a day of school each time we moved. And you need to have a phone so they can get in touch if you're absent, to see what's the matter.

Because of distance, age, or lack of an escort, some homeless children change schools each time they move to a different shelter. With each switch, school records must be transferred and transportation arrangements refigured. And each time the child must readjust to new faces, unfamiliar teachers, and an alien curriculum.

MICHAEL:

How many schools have I been in this year?
Hmmm . . . let me see. My first school, I was living in
our own apartment in Brooklyn. Then we had to move
out, so we went to live with my grandmother and I went
to another school. And then we went to this shelter, so I
went to another school. So this is my third school. We're
moving again next week. I don't know where I'll go to
school.

It's hard starting in the middle of the year. I was
always scared because I didn't know anybody in there.
You know how they stare at you at first. But I always get
friendly with somebody by my fifth day at school.

MARIA P.:

I must have changed schools five times in two years.
I went to school in Brooklyn before we got evicted the
second time. Then I transferred to another school in
Manhattan closer to the shelter. From there I moved
upstate with a friend and I went to high school there.
Then I came back to live with my father in Staten Island
and I went to high school over there. Then I moved back
with my mother when she moved to a hotel, but I kept
going to high school in Staten Island. I would get up at
five o'clock in the morning to leave my house and get on
the ferry. I loved school over there. My best friend
Nadine is there. I didn't want to leave it.

The shelter or hotel environment itself greatly affects how well children do at school.

DOREEN:
It was hard doing homework in the hotel because a lot of times there was too much noise and commotion. I'd tell Mom I did my homework, but I just wouldn't do it. In our room it was too hard. All I had was our one room, and people walking in and out at all times. I wasn't going to do my homework like that. So I just decided to forget it. My grades went down a lot. In seventh grade I was an A student. And in eighth grade, when I was at the hotel, I got a C, an F, and a D.

DENISE:
When we moved from the hotel to [a family-style shelter], my grades started going back up, because we had our own apartment and I could work in the bedroom. And my brother who had dropped out was talking to some counselors there, and they said they could put him in a GED [high school equivalency degree] class. So he's getting his GED now, and they arranged for me to go to a private school.

SONYA:
My sister was always bothering me, so I would go inside the area where the refrigerator was and do my homework. That was the only place in the room to go.

Of course, academic performance suffers as a result of these circumstances. There are homeless students at the top of their class. One study found, though, that the general picture is much bleaker — only 43 percent of homeless students were reading at or above grade level, compared with 68 percent of students citywide. Likewise, only 28 percent of homeless students scored at or above grade level on mathematics ability tests compared with 57 percent citywide.

NAVONNI:
The subject that could keep me back now is math. I got behind when I switched schools. That's what I've got to work on. I hate when I get low scores — I feel bad. I try my best, I'm improving it.

If students can't keep up with their classes, they risk getting left back a grade. Getting left back in school feels like a black mark in the life of any child.

NAVONNI:
In June, by the time I got settled in the hotel, seventh grade was almost over. My mother wanted me to be in school, just to be in there, you know. But they told us, "Don't come here, because we're going to give the seventh graders half days and they aren't going to be in school too much." So my mother told me not to go to school for the rest of the term, and that after Labor Day I'd come back to school. So I missed the last couple weeks of seventh grade.

I was scared I was going to get left back. But they said I'll be put in eighth grade next year. I was so happy. I would have been so mad if I'd have been left back, because it would have messed up my whole record. I NEVER GOT LEFT BACK!! It's important to me because I feel that if you get left back, you're not doing too well in school, there's something wrong. And it just sounds so uneducated, like you don't want to learn. I want to learn.

DENISE:

*I might be left back because I might be eight credits
short. I'm strong, though, to a certain point. I'm not
going to drop out of school; I'm going to keep on trying.
I'm going to summer school. You have no choice. You
have to deal with what happens. I just wish they'd give
you credits for moving around!!*

Given all the obstacles, it is no surprise to learn that
attendance rates for homeless children are much lower
than for others. All too often, homelessness makes it so
hard to get an education that some children drop out altogether. And without even a high school education, the
odds are that the children will never escape the grip of
poverty.

DENISE:

*When we had to move from Queens to Manhattan, my
older brother just forgot about school and dropped out.
He said, "Why should I finish school?" He didn't want to
travel all the way to Queens, and he didn't want to
change his school.*

MARIA P.:

*Between all the school changing my credits were messed
up, and they said I might have to stay back another year.
I didn't know what was going on. So I dropped out and I
started working full-time. Now I'm going to the Job
Corps and I'll make up the credits over there. I'm gonna
try to get the GED. I want to get it over with real soon,
because I want to be a policewoman.*

MARIA O.:

*School is the future. If you give up school, you're giving
up your life. I'll be talking about bums with my teacher*

*sometimes. I'll ask "Why did they become bums?" And
the teacher will say they became bums because they
were acting stupid in school, they laughed too much,
they didn't do their homework; and I say, "That can't be
the problem, how can that be the problem?" And my
teacher said, "Well, that probably isn't the problem. They
probably gave up, they didn't go to college, they didn't
have enough money." So you shouldn't give up school
for something else. You give up school, and you're giving
up your whole life.*

8

Health at Risk

The health of homeless children is, generally speaking, very poor compared to that of other American children. One doctor, who serves children in welfare hotels, feels that many of the children he has seen suffer from the effects of overcrowding, poor nutrition, poor sanitation, and the stress of dislocation. These are conditions associated more often with impoverished nations than with America.

Before coming to New York, he treated uprooted and starving children in Africa: "We don't see the exotic illnesses of the Sudan or Ethiopia, but the high incidences of untreated chronic illnesses and complications, acute illness, and children without immunization, remind me of refugee populations in developing countries. We see children with severe asthma, who are without medicine or proper follow-up. We see children who have hearing difficulties leading to language delay, where the hearing problem is caused by a simple untreated ear infection."

In a country that prides itself on advanced medical technology, thousands of homeless children are at risk of contracting diseases once thought to be virtually vanquished by universal immunization. All American children are supposed to be immunized against diphtheria, tetanus, whooping cough, and polio before they are six months old; and measles, mumps, and German measles before they first attend school. But rates of underimmunization as high as twenty-seven percent have been found in groups of children living in welfare hotels, compared to eight percent for poor children who have homes.

It's easy to see how homelessness can lead to this. Complete immunization requires a series of trips to the doctor, over the course of several years. In the chaos of homelessness, medical appointments that aren't emergencies tend not to happen at all. If children stop going to the same doctor, because they are moving around, it becomes even less likely that their immunization series will be completed. Parents easily lose track of their children's immunization histories and medical records, along with their other possessions.

Homelessness and hunger travel together. Homeless families simply don't get enough to eat while they are moving from place to place. They have little or no money to buy food. Parents skip meals and give all their food to their children, often losing harmful amounts of weight themselves.

A long-term placement in a hotel or shelter does not guarantee that a family gets enough nutritious food to eat. As mentioned in Chapter 4, many welfare hotels have no cooking facilities, and families get a very small "restaurant allowance." Families without cooking facilities are forced to rely on cheap junk food, which does not meet their nutritional needs. Nor can they follow prescribed medical diets, such as low sodium or low fat. Babies cannot be properly fed: bottles need to be sterilized; otherwise babies receive large doses of bacteria with each feeding. This can result in bacterial colonization of the intestine, causing severe diarrhea and dehydration.

The environment a young child lives in has a crucial impact on his or her development. If a living environ-

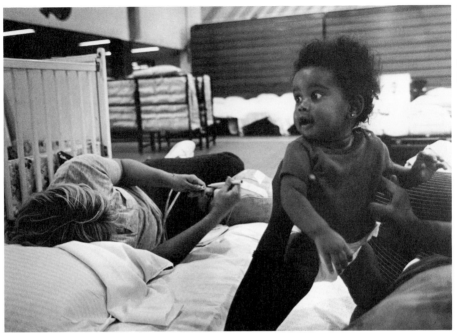

*In barracks-style shelters with beds so close together,
disease easily spreads.*

ment is not suitable for young children, the impact on them
can be alarmingly harmful. Learning how to walk, for example, can be delayed if a child has little space to practice.
Development is also harmed by dislocation, stress, and the
absence of stable relationships. It is no wonder that homeless preschool children, in comparison to poor children who
have homes, have been shown to have much higher rates
of severe delays in language development, in acquiring
motor skills, and in personal/social growth.

Health and development problems can start even before
birth. The general health and nutrition of a pregnant
mother determine, to a large extent, how healthy her baby
will start out life. Homeless families with pregnant mothers,
ironically, tend to be moved by the city from place to place

more often than others — because fewer shelters will accept pregnant women for more than a few days.

The unborn suffer from their mother's deprivation. A doctor who interviewed over a thousand families seeking shelter feels that "City policies and practices for homeless pregnant women are exactly the activities that would provoke premature births and stunted growth of babies. It's not intentional, but that's the outcome when pregnant mothers are carrying luggage and toddlers from place to place . . . , not getting bed rest or proper nutrition." More than twelve percent of homeless pregnant women lose weight, rather than gain it, as their pregnancy proceeds. Hunger, inadequate sleep, and stress take their toll.

Many homeless pregnant women get little or no prenatal care. Not surprisingly, in recent years, low-birth-weight babies have been born to mothers in welfare hotels at a rate more than *twice* that for mothers in the city overall. The infant mortality rate — that sad indicator used to chart a society's standard of living — for children born to homeless women living in hotels is double that for other children in the city.

Basic health care is almost impossible for homeless families to maintain. Once homeless, families leave behind whatever doctors, hospitals, or clinics they may have had. Routine appointments and visits for minor problems tend to be delayed until a situation has become an emergency. Some public health nurses are stationed in the hotels, but they are limited to providing first aid and referrals to local hospitals or clinics. And they are very overworked — each nurse has an enormous caseload. One doctor brings his medical services directly to children, using three vans as mobile doctors' offices. But the vans' staff cannot possibly give complete medical care to every homeless child who needs it.

Medical care is more available in the two kinds of shelters than in the hotels, because state laws require that the shelters have a nurse on duty at all times, and links to local hospitals. Despite this, the barracks-style shelters have perhaps the least healthful environment of all. There, the conditions are so risky that pregnant women, babies under six months old, and people with health problems are forbidden to stay in them.

It is impossible to prevent the spread of disease throughout the crowded sleeping areas and bathrooms of a barracks-style shelter. With dozens of people sleeping head to head in each large room, a single person who comes down with a contagious illness or infection can pass it to many others. There are no "sick rooms" in the shelter where ill people can be quarantined. Unsanitary diaper changing conditions make it even easier for disease to spread, since fecal matter harbors disease-causing germs. Parents typically change diapers in the bathroom sinks in which everyone washes; if these are too crowded, parents change diapers right on their beds.

As a result of these conditions, children and parents living in barracks-style shelters get sick easily and often. A very high percentage come down with such respiratory diseases as influenza and ear infections, and with diarrhea accompanied by vomiting and fever. According to one New York City Department of Health survey, out of all the children living in these shelters, over half of those between the ages of seven months and three years developed diarrhea, and one third of those between the ages of three and six. Diarrhea, as is well known in Third World countries, is very risky for young children. If prolonged, it can lead to dehydration, extreme weight loss and death.

Outbreaks of such highly contagious diseases as measles, mumps, and chicken pox are common in the barracks-style shelters. In fact, measles made its appearance in these shelters years before the current nationwide resurgence. If somebody comes down with such a disease, he or she must immediately be transferred out. By that time, though, others in the shelter would already have been exposed. On occasion, pregnant women and newborns are placed illegally in these shelters and exposed to these diseases, which, for them, are terribly dangerous.

Simply put, homelessness is bad for one's health.

9

Times of Our Lives

ELIZABETH:

Here, at HELP I, they have an art program and I can learn more about drawing. I help draw things, like for a party they're gonna have. But mostly what I do is play basketball a lot in the gym. I'm the only girl . . . I play against the men. I really play good. And I play Ping-Pong. They make teams here for the Little League too. In the summer they're gonna have girls in the Little League. It's really good for the children. People say you never get bored in here because there's always something to do.

TRACY:

I read in a newspaper once that play time is the most important time of a child's life. So I like to do a lot of the things here. In the activity center, they have arts and crafts, music, Black poetry reading, African dancing. I like that, 'cause they play drums for us to dance to. We make bracelets and make pictures they hang up. Every Saturday we come down here and do one of those things. And there's a playground right here outside our room so we don't have to worry about going to a park or anywhere.

The luck of the draw determines whether homeless children stay at a place that's well-equipped with things for them to do. Some shelters, especially those run by nonprofit organizations, have recreational activities and programs to help children improve their prospects for the future.

KWAZEE:
They give some of the kids jobs in here. Now I'm a counselor. I take little kids to the movies or to the park, or help them with their homework, or talk to them and stuff. I get $80 every two weeks working every day after school. It's called "work readyness," and they're preparing us for the real world and a real job after we leave here.

Most shelters, though, are not nearly so geared to the needs of older children. Welfare hotels are not required to provide any activities for children at all. To make matters worse, many shelters and hotels are in the midst of drug-infested neighborhoods, far from safe parks, or in business districts. Many children have no break from the tension of homelessness.

JIMMY:
The hotel is so aggravating. You can't go nowhere, move around. There are no hang-out places. You can't have company, because there isn't enough room. You have to go hang out in the hallways.

YVETTE:
I don't go down into the street to play, because there is no place to play on the streets. The streets are dangerous because there are all kinds of people who are on drugs or crazy.

Chaos and stress without end can sap energy, dull motivation, and make one feel listless and numb.

DOREEN:
When I was in the hotel, I would stay up on my bed with my books and my stuffed animals. I had really little energy, and I really didn't feel like doing much. I would read, and then I would go to sleep. And that would be the end of my day.

TASHA:
My little brother and sister don't come out of the room now. They go to school, come in, go out, don't say "Hi" to nobody. They just play with their toys, or watch TV.

MICHAEL:
When I get up on weekends, sometimes I just keep my pajamas on. And my mother's boyfriend always tells me to put on some clothes. I don't know for what. He says maybe I might have to go to the store or something. So I put on my clothes, and we don't do nothing. We just sit and play in the hallway. I wasted these clothes just to do nothing?

SHAMA:
I was so bored in the hotel, because my mother didn't let us do anything. She was afraid to let us out of the room. We had a small TV that we watched on the bed.

Activities are provided in a few of the hotels by nonprofit volunteer groups. They are most welcome.

NAVONNI:
They have groups at the hotel that take kids on trips to

places they've never been to. I went white-water rafting, inner tubing, canoeing. It was so much fun because it was something I never did before. Inner tubing, now that was fun. All of them was fun for me. At least I got a chance now to say I went. I can say, "I went canoeing, I went white-water rafting."

"Oasis Rap"

At Oasis club we do art,
We go to the library, we go to the park.
On Saturdays we head outside.
We take lots of trips with a subway ride.
  We exercise, can't you see?
  We work out to be as healthy as can be.
  We get picked up each and every day,
  We learn to read in an awesome way.
We put up a Learning Tree,
So we could learn to Read Read Read!
OASIS. OASIS! It's better than other places.

In the summertime, most homeless children are limited by poverty to the sweltering city.

TASHA:
On the weekends, during the summertime, we be dancing outside the hotel. People would be out on the sidewalk with the drums and the radio, and we started talking to them. They asked my little brother to dance and make a couple of dollars. I remember the first time they asked me to dance. I was shy in front of boys. I was like, "Me, really?" There were six of us, three boys, three girls. It was so much fun.

93

Children and volunteers painting a mural on a building wall

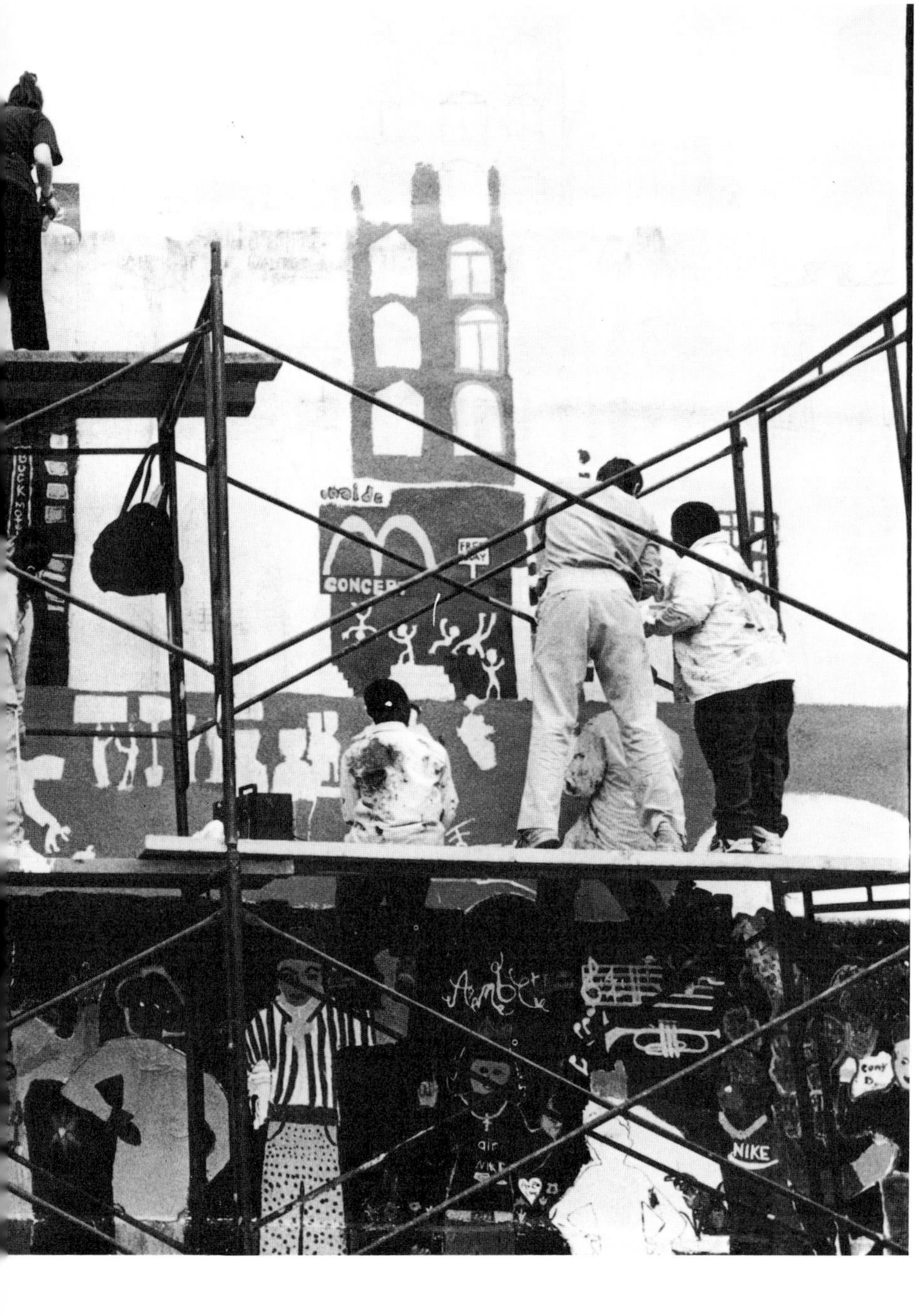

Maria Corley

Some children are lucky enough to live in a shelter or hotel where they can hook up with a summer program. A few nonprofit organizations run sleep-away camps for homeless children. The camps resemble summer camps everywhere, except that most of the children have never been to a camp before. Many have never even been out of the city.

LEON:
The thing I like about camp is that everyone is like a family. We're always doing something. There's no fights, no bums, and no shoot-outs. And the city has all those things.

DOUGLAS:
I came to camp because I knew it would be fun. Another reason I came to camp was to get out of the city. The city is real noisy at night, and camp is so quiet that you could hear a raccoon run through the woods. In the city you'll be lucky to hear yourself talk.

> *Camp Homeward Bound has found the sound*
> *To make all kids come gather round*
> *And get up on the fresh*
> *Homeward Bound Sound.*

Children have the opportunity to do things they might never do otherwise.

MARIA O.:
When I first came to camp, I hated the first thing we had to do, canoeing. My arms were killing me! I said, "Oh God, I don't deserve this kind of stuff. I don't deserve it!" And when I first saw the director, I said,

"Please don't put me in a bunk with this girl Angela. She's my enemy from the shelter!" He said that would probably change in two weeks. And it changed. Me and her aren't enemies no more.

MELANIE:
When we went camping we ate different foods like Indian food, French food, and we learned how to say "I love you" in French. I'm not so crazy about cleaning the toilet bowls 'cause they are so smelly! The counselors treat you very nice. You can talk to them about anything, and even about boys.

JOHNNY:
I love nature. Grass, trees, lakes. I liked when we went hiking. When we were walking, it wasn't too fun. But afterwards it was fun. We sat on this rock and started fishing. I love fishing. That's my favorite thing to do.

It was sad at the end of camp. The next morning we were going to go. We had a dance in the "rec" hall — when the slow dance music came on, all the little girls started crying, and then my dance partner was crying. Everybody was sad. Some people didn't want to dance, they just wanted to sit there and cry.

10

Who Am I Now? Homelessness and Identity

KWAZEE:
*When we had to leave my aunt's, I was scared. I thought
we were gonna be on the streets like I had seen
homeless people. You see it on TV and you never think it
would happen to you.*

What does it mean to be "homeless"? The expression describes the circumstance of not having a permanent place to live. Often misunderstood, though, is how someone can have a roof over his or her head, and still be considered "homeless." Having a place other than the streets to stay for the night is fundamentally different from having one's own home.

DENISE:
*If you don't have your own apartment, it doesn't feel
right. You don't feel whole. When you have your own
apartment, you feel happier — like you are your own
boss. You don't have to listen to nobody, you can just go
in your room and shut the door when you're mad, and
get away from it all. You have privacy. It's hard to
explain.*

The word *homeless* applies both to families who live in shelters and to the men and women who live in public places. Some homeless children empathize with the plight of street people; others do not want to be associated with them.

MARIA O.:
I see all those people out there, the bums, I see them
trying and trying. I see a lot of bums around the shelter,
and they take the food out of the trash, and I say to
myself, "Why can't they have a bed and sleep in a warm
place?" Sometimes I used to cry because of that. I'm
homeless too, but I just can't help them, and I wish I
could help them.

SHEBA:
They should use another word besides homeless.
Homeless *makes me think of the people living in the*
street, begging for money. That's what they want to do
with their lives. They don't want to try to survive, to
make it. We shouldn't be called the same thing as them.

Homeless children do not think of themselves as essentially different from children with homes.

TRACY:
At the shelter we live almost like normal people who
have their own house. We just don't have a place to live
and that's the only problem with us. We don't do
anything different from you or anybody else.

KAREEM:
The shelter is only another home, it's not another life.
It's not like I just moved into another life like an alien, or

99

something like that. I can move into a sewer, and still
stay the same person. The shelter doesn't control who
you are.

SHEBA:
There's no difference between you living on Park Avenue
and me living at the Prince George Hotel. Both of us
have a roof over our heads. It's just that you're more able
to do what you want to do. You might have more money,
so you can go out and buy yourself a pair of shoes and
new clothes. I can't do that. But I can go out with my
friends the same amount that you do. I don't consider
myself "homeless." Just unable to get myself out of the
situation that I'm in. I have no apartment, but I have a
roof over my head.

Becoming homeless, though, may change how other people view a child. Attached to the word *homeless* are derogatory connotations that often have little to do with reality, yet they stick to a person like a label. Terms like *vagrant, derelict,* and *bum* are frequently used to describe street people. The stigma attached to homeless street people can rub off on homeless children, even though their circumstances are different.

KWAZEE:
People would look at me because of the way I'd be
dressed — sharp. Some of my friends, when I tell them
I'm homeless, they're shocked because I don't act like
I'm homeless. They think if you're homeless, you have to
look poor or dress like a bum. But that's not the case. My
mother always said, "You got clothes, keep them clean —

100

Being homeless makes many children feel ashamed.

so you feel good about yourself and people will respect you."

While clean clothes may be a matter of effort, *new* clothes are a luxury beyond the means of most homeless children. Having a very limited wardrobe is one aspect of being poor, which embarrasses many children. And in a society that values and celebrates affluence, being poor can in itself feel like a mark of disgrace.

JIMMY:
Living in a hotel makes you feel low, because everybody knows it's a welfare hotel, and everybody knows that everyone in there is on welfare. It's degrading.

KAREEM:
If being a poor child living in a rich city is a crime, then I'm guilty. I don't steal, rob people, use drugs, stay out all night, or play hooky from school. People have no right to punish me for something I have no control over. I keep telling myself that I don't deserve this.

The attitudes others have about homeless children can and do affect how they feel about themselves.

JENELLE:
They have 6:00 P.M. meetings sometimes at the shelter, where they ask the kids, "How do you feel being here?" I say, "I feel mad, because I don't like people seeing me going into this building." Other people have homes. They might say, "See that girl over there, she don't got a home." They'd go behind your back. They might say, "She's homeless because her mother is poor." And I'll be getting mad. The whole thing makes me want to fight.

Perhaps the hardest place to be while homeless is at school.

DOREEN:
They still don't know at school. I won't tell them. They would spread vicious rumors about me. They'd say, "Oh, she lives in a hotel. Her mother must not be able to take care of her. She's probably selling her body to get food." I've seen them torment other kids. This one girl was living in a hotel, and somebody had taken a Barbie doll and they had a Ken doll wrapped around it. They wrote "slut" on it, and said, "Ah hah, we know that you live in a hotel." And they threw it in her locker. I remember she went home crying that day.

102

SHAMA:

I didn't want to tell my friends at school, because who wants to tell people that they live in such a bad place? And so, I would just say I lived in the building where my aunt's friend lives.

JOSÉ:

We were on the school bus, and this lady asked this girl from the shelter, "Where do you live?" She lied and said she lived in an apartment. So I asked her, "Why did you lie?" She said, "You want me to tell her where we live?" I said, "I don't care." Who knows if maybe that lady wanted to visit her sometime? So that day, that girl did wrong, because she was lying.

BURTON:

One of the guys told me that one of the girls teasing me about living in the hotel was living in a hotel too! I think she just teased me because she wanted the guys to laugh at her jokes.

Even those who are top students fear receiving negative attention.

SHEBA:

What bad could they say? I'm an A student, I'm on the honor roll, I'm very active. They can't say I'm in the hotel because I'm dumb. But I still don't want anyone to know in my school, because they'll always be talking about it. Even if I move out to my own home, it won't matter. Everyone will continue talking about this same situation over and over behind my back.

Despite children's best attempts to hide that they are

homeless, sometimes a school's practices make it obvious to everyone.

MICHAEL:
Kids from the hotel can't bring home other kids from school, because the people from the hotel have to leave earlier to get on the bus to go home. The principal would say, "People from the bus get ready and come with me."

JACKIE:
When we went to school, they took all the hotel children and put us in one classroom. The fourth grade was with the fifth grade. They just put us in one big room. All of us went into one gym and all the others went into the other gyms they had in the school. They just put all the hotel children in one big gym. They separated us from the other kids. The teachers weren't saying anything. They were just doing their jobs. Some of the parents got together and made the school stop doing that.

Switching schools is a rough time for anyone, but it can be even harder if one is both the "new kid" and a "homeless kid" at the same time.

DENISE:
I started at my new school at the end of October. I didn't like going to school, I guess, because I didn't know anybody there. I just sat by myself and copied everything off the board. No one would talk to me. I didn't really care. Well, I did sort of. I'm not used to making new friends.

Some homeless children just don't let the negative expectations others have about them get under their skin. Others can't help it.

MARIA O.:
You shouldn't be ashamed to tell people you live in a shelter. If someone doesn't want to be your friend just because you live in a shelter, that's silly. You're homeless, and you gotta just learn to live with it. It's not funny, and it's not a game.

NAVONNI:
It doesn't make a difference if you're homeless or not. All you have to like about a person is how they are. How they react to you. Now, if they act all stinky and stuck up, then you stay away from them. But if I act nice to you, I expect you to act nice to me. If I respect you, I expect you to respect me too.

KAREEM:
It's strange, but I really like when the lights go off in the movies because then I'm no longer a "homeless kid." I'm just a person watching the movie like everyone else.

A lot of the children at the hotel believe that they are "hotel kids." They've been told by so many people for so long that they are not important, that they live up to what is expected of them. It gets so some children have no dreams and live in a nightmare because they believe that they are "hotel kids." It's worse than being in jail. In jail you can see the bars and you know when you're getting out. In the hotel you can't see the bars because they're inside of you and you don't know when you're getting out.

11

The Endurance Test: Living with Stress

NAVONNI:
My mother gets sick because she worries so much about how she's going to get an apartment. Sometimes we get on her nerves, and her nerves are very bad. She had a headache for about two or three weeks.

The strain of homelessness deeply affects each family member, and how they all get along together. Parents must always worry about how and where to find a permanent home, and what they will do once they find one. At the same time, they must worry about their immediate situation: where their children will go to school or to daycare, how they will be able to buy enough food, clothes, diapers, or subway fare on their very small budget, and every other aspect of their family's well-being.

They worry about all of these things, but they have little control over them. Parents are no longer the ultimate authority figure in the lives of their children. Instead, a faceless "system" is calling the shots. It's a heavy load, which takes its toll on parents' physical and emotional health. Children, in turn, are affected by everything their parents go through.

NAVONNI:

I can't be under as much stress as my mother is under. The only person I got to really worry about is me. My mother has to worry about all of us, got to think for all of us, got to feed all of us. I don't have to do that much.

MARIA P.:

My mother kind of freaked out. She started getting freaky because all the yelling around the hotel gets you nervous. Like when you're sleeping, and all of a sudden you hear a yell and screams and then shots and you don't know where it's coming from. Now she's quieter, but before she would yell at us for no reason. She said we'd be out of there soon and not to worry — she was working hard to get us out. And she did work really hard to get us out of there, and she finally did.

JOSÉ:

When my mother gets nervous, I get nervous. And I get scared when she gets scared. I try to calm her down.

Living crowded for a long period of time — in a tiny hotel room, or a large room surrounded by strangers — can cause tension in a family.

MARIA P.:

When we lived in one room, we got so tired of seeing each other's faces that we'd fight and argue over the TV and stuff. Everybody just became wacko and started acting crazy. The second year we were there, my little sister ran away for a month. We searched for her everywhere, and my mother got a police warrant on her and we couldn't find her. That's when things were really bottom up. Right now I'm nervous just thinking about that. It was quite an experience.

DENISE:
*My mother really wasn't used to the situation, with so
many people in one room, and no kitchen or privacy or
anything. She was used to going to work, coming home,
cooking dinner, cleaning up, looking at TV. She didn't
like having to deal with so many people she didn't know
all the time. The whole family was arguing, all the kids
against the mother.*

Some children feel angry and let down by their parents
because they are homeless.

SHEBA:
*At the beginning I was angry at my mother, but well, it's
been done already. I can't hold on to it. I try not to put it
on my mother. It comes back to me sometimes, though.
I'll say I'll never do this. I can't really say never, because
it can always happen to me, but I will try never to have
my family in this situation in the future.*

On the other hand, living through the stress of homelessness can bring some families closer together. Isolated
from the usual sources of moral support, like friends, relatives, neighbors, or church, each family member is more
dependent than ever upon the others. Times of crisis can
illuminate the meaning of family bonds.

KWAZEE:
*When we moved from place to place, we had to stick
close together, and it built us up. It made us become
stronger, because we were all that we had. My family*

pulled together with each other. We had hard times, but having the love for one another, I didn't really feel too bad because we had each other.

NAVONNI:
My mother tells us all the time, "We have to stick together as a family. No matter what. Because we need each other." She says she's not gonna have us disrespecting each other or fighting. We're supposed to love each other like a family. "And if you can't do that, it's just too bad, because as long as you're with me you're gonna obey my rules."

"Who Cares" by Sharneen

*Nobody really cares
anymore but me
No one wants to cry for me
Nobody wants to care for me
   Who will sit down and then
   Stand up for me
   Nobody cares anymore but me
Who cares for me
My mother
She helps me solve my problems
and we share our love
We tell each other things
My brother cares to share our love
   I really fight for people who care about me
   My beautiful mother
   And my brother*

LEON:
I used to think my father was perfect, and I still think

Isolated from friends and other sources of support, each family member depends more than ever upon the others.

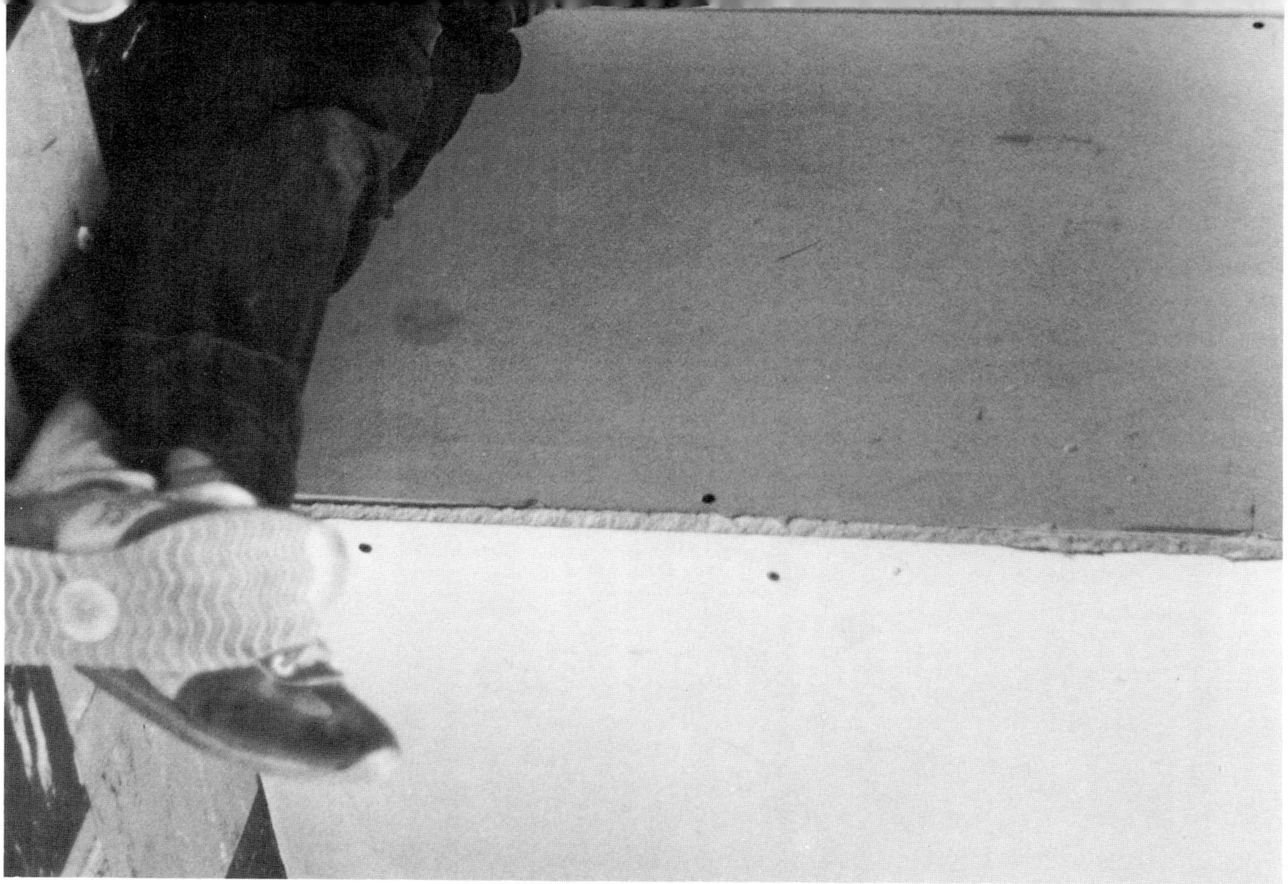

Laurel Danowitz

he's perfect in a way. He's my role model. He keeps us all together. My father is the only person I can really trust right now, besides my brothers. He's lived longer than me and experienced more, so I look up to him. If I have a question, I'll just go to my father. He knows everything.

JOSÉ:
We take care of each other good. My big brother, he's nice to me. He'll see that I don't have anything to do, he gives me money, or he'll say, "Let's go to the store." He wants me to feel good, and my mother does too.

One of the first things my mother likes about me is I respect her. When sometimes I say something wrong to my mother, I feel bad. I feel like my mother's getting a bad feeling in her heart.

KWAZEE:
I talk a lot to my sister, who's just a year older than me. Like the first time we became homeless, when I was ten. I didn't really understand what was happening — sometimes I would cry because I didn't understand. And then I started reading about it and I would talk to my sister, and we would cry and try to understand everything, because you need to feel comfortable with somebody. I could only talk to my family — I couldn't talk to anybody else. And sometimes I still kept things inside.

NAVONNI:
When I know my mother's under a lot of stress, I tell her, "Why don't you come talk to me?" So my mother really talks to me the most. Sometimes I talk to my mother, sometimes I don't like to talk to my mother, not

*because she wouldn't want to listen, but because she
wouldn't understand.*

Some parents, in reaction to homelessness, become much more protective of their children, especially if they are living in a dangerous environment. At the same time, the universal law that teenagers will struggle for independence still applies.

NAVONNI:
*I don't want my mother to always help me. I'm a big girl
now, and I'm supposed to know how to manage things
on my own. I'll be a teenager before you know it.
Thirteen, fourteen's gonna come up. Soon I'll be in high
school. High school sounds so big to me.*

DOREEN:
*Kids need to have their parents let them grow.
Sometimes my mother can't separate herself from me.
I tell her, "No matter how much you tell me not to
explore, I'm going to."*

SHEBA:
*Teenagers are going to do something wrong. They're
going to experiment and experience. That's what
teenagers do.*
   *I've seen my little brother go through changes. He
thinks he's the man of the place now. He wants to go
look for a job. He wants to perform, he likes to go out
and experience things, so he will know. And if he likes
something, he goes back. I tell him to relax, and be a kid
as long as he can. He says, "I know everything!" I say,
"No, you don't."*

MARIA P.:

How a kid turns out is really all up to the kid and the parent. If the parent explains things and tries to be more like a friend than a parent, then the kid understands that you're not telling them what to do, that you're trying to help them make their own choice, it's their life. Some parents try to pressure you to be a certain individual, but you can't be. A lot of times I think that's what makes kids go the wrong way.

Children, especially teenagers, want and need to have ties with people outside the family. Staying in touch with old friends while living through the chaos of homelessness, though, can be difficult.

JIMMY:

Your friends can't get in touch with you. In some hotels, you don't even have a place where your mail comes. Our hotel room didn't have a phone for a year. I would run into my old friends on the street, get their phone numbers, and call them from a phone booth. We used to go and visit them, and tell them how it was in the hotel, and they'd wish us luck getting out of there.

KWAZEE:

When you're around a lot of friends, it makes you feel good. You move to a different neighborhood, and you have to make new friends. It's hard to move around and always have to make new friends.

Friendships themselves may be affected by the circumstances. It's possible that an old friend may not want to stay friends with someone who has become homeless. A true friendship, though, will survive; a true friend will help lighten the load.

MARIA O.:
Every time I'd go to the pool, I'd see friends who didn't know I lived in a shelter. It got to the point where I told them, and they said, "It's cool, we can still be friends."

KWAZEE:
Right now I am homeless, but I have a lot of friends. They know my situation, and they don't put me down or anything — they don't make me feel homeless.

"The Friendship Song" by Carrie

Forever and ever
I'll be your friend until ever more
Through good times and bad times
you can count on me forever more.
  Be a friend, be a friend to each other
  Be a big sister and a brother
  Be a friend to me that's all I ask
Be a friend to everyone you meet
on the street
just like me

In addition to family and friends, faith helps some children through the hard times.

JOSÉ:
My mother really believes in God. Today we went to church, and she heard a song they played when her father died, so she started crying. Every time we go to church, she lights a candle and makes a wish. They say that if you go to church, your dreams will come true. I don't really believe that, but it's good going to church. I like it.

Homelessness can illuminate the meaning of family bonds.

NAVONNI:
*I believe that God will bless you to succeed in everything
you do, and give you everlasting life. You've got to be
very unlucky to get hurt.*

SHEBA:
*The Prince George Hotel has the devil all through the
place. So you have to sing something different than what
they are listening to. I like to sing gospel at the shows
they have in the ballroom. The people really listen — like
they've never heard anything like it before. I feel good
about it. The Lord is with me, and that makes me feel
good. He is singing through me. They need it. It makes*

me feel better because I'm singing for the Lord. It gives Him less to do.

If I could have one wish, it would be something crazy, like everyone in the hotel would go to Radio City Music Hall and listen to gospel all night, and the ministers would be singing this song:
I know somehow, I know some way,
We're gonna make it.
No matter what the test, no matter what comes our way,
We're gonna make it.
With Jesus on our side,
Things will work out all right,
We're gonna make it.

Others find themselves questioning their beliefs.

MARIA P.:
I was really angry. I felt like I did something really, really wrong to go through what I did, that I sinned, that it was some kind of punishment or test from God. But then I would feel guilty, because it could have been worse, like living on the street. I thank God that we didn't have to live on the street, or on a corner, or in a box like a lot of homeless people.

Living in the hotel and the shelter did change how I felt about God, in a way. I feel that there has to be some kind of strength to have helped us get through what we went through. I feel there's a higher being up there that helped us get to where we are now, and blessed us with being healthy and everything. Sometimes I believed less in Him, but I still believed.

Homelessness is a test of morale for parents as well as children. There are some parents who radiate hope and strength, bolstering the spirits of their family and those around them. There are others who become demoralized. The fact that they have children may be all that keeps them going.

ANGELA:
My mother said to the three of us: "Angie, if you die, Laura and Steven won't have a mother, because I'll kill myself." She told Laura, "If you die, Angie and Steven won't have a mother because I'll kill myself." And she told Steven, "If you die, your sisters won't have a mother because I'll kill myself." She's got to live her life with all three of us. That's it. Without us three, she won't know how to live her life no more. She might get on drugs, she wouldn't know what to do.

Some parents lose hope and the will to survive altogether, escaping from reality through drug or alcohol abuse. At the worst point, not even their children remain incentives to keep going.

JIMMY:
When you first get to the hotel, you're all right. But living there deteriorates some people. I've seen parents who are sober at first, and then they start smoking crack and stuff like that. I've seen families break up, literally, because their mothers started smoking drugs.

DOREEN:
There was a boy who used to live at the hotel whose mother got addicted to crack. At one point she was probably one of the best mothers in the world, before she found crack. You can just tell from the way her son is. He would say, "Yes, ma'am," and "No, ma'am," to my

118

Friends make it easier to bear.

mother, and "Yes, sir," and "No, sir," to my father. He was
always very nice. At some point last year he started stealing,
so he could get money, so they could eat. Because she was
spending all their money on crack. It wasn't good that he
was stealing, but at least he was trying to get food.

SHAMA:
The parents that did drugs, their kids were always
playing out in the hallways, or running around on the
stairs. Day and night. This boy David, he didn't even
know where his mother was. At two or three in the
morning, he would still be in the hallway. He was
twelve. My mother asked him once, "Where's your
mother?" He said, "I don't know, I don't know." She was
out all night.

When the unpleasantness of a situation becomes over-
whelming, children, too, can be tempted to escape from
reality.

MARIA P.:
Before we moved to the hotel, my little sister was real
quiet and kept to herself, and didn't mess with drugs or
anything. Then she started hanging out inside the hotel
and she started smoking weed and who knows what
else. One day she came home and I smelled reefer on
her. I wanted to kill her. But then I started doing it
myself. Why? I wouldn't say that I liked it. I didn't like
the smell or the taste of it — it was disgusting. Maybe it
was just for the fun of it. It was boring in the hotel. It
made me feel a little better sometimes.

The most potent weapon children have against despair comes from within: a strong sense of themselves.

AKHEEM:
I kept myself from being unhappy by finding my own things to do. I wasn't staying in the hotel all the time. I would go outside. I just didn't hang out there.

MARIA P.:
Everybody started going their own way after a while. I started going out a lot more and hanging out by the East River, just to get away from that environment. I used to sit on the benches and look into the sea and just think.

SHAMA:
I kept reminding myself to think that it was only a temporary situation — we're not going to stay there for a long time. I didn't know we would be there for a whole year. You have to really be there to understand it.

DENISE:
I keep more to myself. I like to sit home and read books. I love books. I don't like to follow people and pick up their habits. I like to be myself and pick the right friends. You have to keep your own mind.

DOREEN:
If I don't like what's around me I change it. I find friends that I like. I seek out people who like me.

KAREEM:
I would go in the hallway and make a few friends, and not bother anybody. You had to say no to everybody, don't use drugs, don't mess with anything, it was hard to

do that. I didn't have that many fights though, I made friends with most of the kids. I coped with it that way — by making friends.

If it's too much for you to handle, the only thing I can say is, just don't give up. Don't let it be that you're a "shelter kid"; let it be that you're a kid in a shelter.

12

Dreams and Visions

Like all children, homeless children have dreams for the future, and wishes for the present. And plenty of opinions, if the President of the United States or the mayor of New York City were to ask them for advice.

What Do I Want to Do When I'm Older?

TRACY:

I asked my mother how much jobs can people have and she says as many as they want. And I told her that when I grow up I'm gonna have at least three jobs, so I can help pay the bills for her and things like that, and give her money if she needs it. I would be a doctor, and I would probably be a policewoman, and I don't know what the third job would be. I told my mother I wanted to be a doctor because I like to help people, like if I see somebody sick on the street I would help them. If somebody gets hurt at school I'm always the first one to be there. I always try to help them and get them to the nurse.

MICHAEL:

I want to get me a job, so I can get money, then I can get a place to stay, then when I get more and more and

*more and more money, I can give some to my mother
and my aunts and cousins and everyone, and then I'll
keep working 'til I get me a whole lot of money.*

JENELLE:
*When I grow up I want to be rich. My mother says, "Oh
yeah, are you going to come back and get me?" I say,
"No, but I'll mail you some money."*

JOSÉ:
*I want to be in the navy, or the air force. I want to fly
jets.*

MARIA O.:
*First I want to go to college, then I want to go to the
academy to be a cop, then if I don't become a cop, a
singer, or a dancer.*

ANGELA (Maria O.'s best friend):
*When I'm big, I want to be a cop, and a singer, or a
dancer. I want to stop all the drugs.*

JACKIE:
*Being a kid is easy, 'cause you think you can do
anything. When you grow up, it's really hard. I don't
want kids when I grow up 'cause I think it's too hard. I
don't want to grow up and do all a that stuff. Being a kid
is fun, and I don't want to stop having fun.*

NAVONNI:

I wanna be a star, everybody crowding around me, and going crazy over me. I just like the feel of it. It's fun, everybody wanting your autograph.

JOHNNY:

My brothers and I are going to be rap artists. We've been singing and dancing together for a while. We perform all over.

AKHEEM:

A star; an actor or a singer, or football. Law seems pretty boring, but it makes a lot of money. I would like to go into the courts and defend someone or prosecute someone.

LEON:

When I grow up I want to be a reporter. Because they get to travel and meet people.

JIMMY:

I don't really know right now, be a chef maybe, or work with kids as a counselor.

KWAZEE:

My football coach works at the shelter, and he was telling me I should go to college.

DENISE:

I want to be a veterinarian and do acting on the side. I had a career — I was accepted into an acting agency. But when we became homeless, I couldn't join the agency — because they wanted $600 for acting school *and pictures. I was mad. But I'm going to work this summer and use the money I make to go back to them, and do it that way.*

ELIZABETH:
I'm starting criminal law in high school. Maybe I want to study law, if I graduate. If I can't, I want to go into the army. My uncle's in the army, and he talks to me about it and he says it's a good place to go. I think I would like it — I really want to go. Maybe in there you can be something better. If I can't go to the army, I would like to be a policewoman or something.

NEWPORT:
I want to be a rap artist — somebody important that people respect.

MARIA P.:
Now I know I want to be a narc, because I've seen drug dealers and I know how they work. They're sneaky; I know how they think. I want to get the drugs out and make it a safer community.

Being sixteen at a welfare hotel was hard, because that's the point in time when you don't know what you want to do. You have to make a lot of decisions, but mostly you have to think about yourself in that particular situation. It was pretty hard.

If I Could Have One Wish:

MICHAEL:
If I could have one wish, it would be for a million dollars. I would share it with my family and my generation. But first I'd get me a house. I would get a house that would

just be for us and nobody else. I haven't had that kind of house for a long time. In fact, I've never had it. My mother already bought a washing machine — I would put it in there. She bought a lot of stuff which she put in storage. When we get our house, we'll take our stuff from out of storage.

KWAZEE:
I would get a big piece of land for myself. And a real big house, like eighteen rooms and fifteen bathrooms.

DENISE:
I would have two closets full of clothes. I love to dress up. I would buy my mother a diamond ring, because she loves jewelry.

TASHA:
I always told my friends that when I move into an apartment, I'll have white couches. I'm gonna live in a penthouse. Like on TV. Stereos — stereo in the kitchen, stereo in the bathroom. I feel that if you wish for something that you really want and you go to school, get a job, do things right, don't be on drugs, if you really want it, you can get all of that. So I have the feeling I will get all of that.

ANGELA:
I want to have my own room and play Nintendo again.

JENELLE:
I want a house where they don't tell you you can't run around.

NAVONNI:

I wish that time could go back and Adam and Eve could do the right thing so this world wouldn't be so evil. I wish there would be no guns in this world, and nothing that can hurt you. That is what I wish.

And I wish that right now everyone could get along together and there would be no more racism. What is there about black people that white people do not like? If I was to go and turn white, people would like me just because my skin is white? Or because of who I am? I don't care who is my friend, I like them for who they are.

TIPHANY:

I drew a picture once of cabins out in the country in the olden days, and a sight of beautiful birds with the sun rising. Also a lake with swans and wind blowing sand. This is a place where I would like to live, with no trouble or violence.

"Somewhere Special" by Maria P.

Earth is a place between heaven and hell
A place where only you decide where you'd go.
I wish there was a place as peaceful as can be
With all the trees and birds as beautiful as a breeze.
The warmth of the sun and sudden fall of rain
That keeps me wanting to live through all the filth and pain.
Every day so pretty, all the nights are through.
I look and smile as the sky is silky blue.
The pain of Sorry surpassed and life so bright with glee:
I wish there was a place where I would like to be.

"The Street of Dreams — Calle de Sueños," a mural painted by homeless children in an arts workshop

Advice to the President and the Mayor:

SHAMA:
If I was President, I would pull down all the shelters.

MICHAEL:
I would tell President Bush that people at the hotel need money. That's for sure. They need a house to stay in instead of staying in that junky place, because it's a wreck.

JOSÉ:
I would say to the mayor they need better food in the shelter, because some people are starving, and they need some electrical outlets.

TASHA:
They should get the addresses of apartments and put them in a book. At work I could make some copies, and I would hand them out to people who need them. That's what they should do.

MARIA P.:
There's a lot of people who want to help. They should have a program to get people materials and stuff so they can fix up these abandoned buildings. That way, the city doesn't have to spend so much money for workers and stuff.

LEON:
They should make the empty lots into buildings or parks. When I was small, I used to think that the President, if he ordered something, he could get it free. I used to think, "Why can't he just tell people to build a building

right across the street in the lot where they just throw trash?" But now I know even the government got to pay to build something.

AKHEEM:

The problem is the city doesn't have the money to put all hotel residents in apartments. So people who have money should help out more and give some money for the homeless people. That's what I think taxes are for.

KWAZEE:

If I had a million bucks, I wouldn't give it to the city — I don't think they know what to do with money. They put it to stupid things that's not helping people. They waste money. In some places they rip down old buildings and put up condominiums and stuff that's too expensive and some people can't afford that. If they build more apartments that people can afford to live in, there'd be less homeless people.

NEWPORT:

I would say to Mr. Bush, it seems like the government is not doing anything. If the government was doing something, you'd see people outside right now with bags picking up the garbage, taking homeless people to restaurants, giving them something to eat. If I was the mayor of New York, I would tax every rich person in the city three dollars for everything they buy. All that money would go back to the homeless. I would build a hundred big, tall buildings only for homeless people, with a big playground. I would take them places. There would be no more trash in the streets. All the streets would be clean, even in the ghetto. There would be no prejudice either. They should let me be the mayor. I would do it right.

131

JIMMY:

They should sit down and think before they give something to a family — is it going to be good or bad for them? If a family really needs something, they should get it, but if they can get it on their own instead, they should. If I was on welfare I'd want to get me a job, so I could do for me, and not have everybody else do for me all the time. The city should open up more daycare centers for mothers on welfare so they can try to find a job and make a living.

TRACY:

I would tell the President that they should tear down all the crack houses, and build a real house where people who are homeless could live, and they would provide food for them if they could not afford to buy things. And they could do anything they wanted, and they wouldn't have any rules and be restricted. You're American, you're free. I would make sure that they would have the best life that they could ever have.

13

The End of the Tunnel

America has long had the reputation of being a "land of opportunity," a cliché that leaves unmentioned the struggles of thousands of its children. Not long ago, the plight of children in homeless families was seen as a national disgrace by the general public, requiring urgent action. Major magazines featured cover stories about them; rock concerts devoted their proceeds to them. Politicians vowed to make helping them a top priority. The attention has died down with the 1990s, even though there are no fewer homeless families in this country today.

But now there are more shelters. If homeless families have shelters and hotels to stay in, the illusion is created that their problems are being taken care of. As the children quoted throughout this book poignantly attest, the reality is to the contrary: their needs are not being met. Shelters and hotels can never take the place of a stable home, and they were never intended to. But, in the absence of a national effort to find solutions to homelessness, shelters and hotels have become housing, by another name, for America's poorest families. Through the eyes of the children here, we can see how the poorest are being treated.

It's hard to understand how such an affluent society could produce so many poor families in need of housing and so much else, and do so little to help them. Home-

lessness, after all, is an aspect of poverty, which affects not thousands, but millions of Americans. Its economic, political, and social causes have been debated for decades. One thing is certain: unless and until the underlying problems are tackled, the shelters will always have a fresh supply of poor families.

Some pieces of the solution are obvious. The federal and local governments could commit themselves to creating much more low-income housing, so that poor families would have alternatives to the shelters. The economic fabric of poor communities could be strengthened, so that families could have opportunities to help themselves. There are political, social, and many other strategies to use in approaching the problem. Make no mistake, it will take an incredible commitment of brainpower, money, and effort to come up with effective answers and put them into action, even more than it took to fight the recent Persian Gulf war. But this country, which can mobilize itself to fight a war on the other side of the world, has demonstrated that it can make a national effort when it wants to. The first step we have to take is to care.

In the year and a half following my research, the children I interviewed scattered all over the city. Some of their families were lucky enough to find permanent housing. The neighborhoods they now live in are amongst the poorest and most dangerous in the city, but the stability of their situations has enabled me to keep in touch with them. In some of these families, the children are managing to get on with the rest of their lives, and are thriving. In others, though, their education, or their morale, have been damaged beyond the point of repair.

MARIA P.:

We moved to our own apartment in the Bronx six months ago. The Bronx is something sort of like a hotel, because there's still drugs and shootings almost every day. It's true everybody needs a nice healthy apartment to live in and grow in. But it's also another thing that if you throw them all in a messed up area, they're gonna come out messed up no matter how hard you try.

When we moved, it opened me up more. That's when I started writing a lot more poems. I got to see how it was being in a hotel and being out of there. It sure feels better to have room for yourself. I guess that's what we needed, some room.

JIMMY:

I feel like I've recovered sometimes. But now I see the homeless people — we were like that once. It's like a scar that you will carry for the rest of your life. I know how it feels.

Many of the other families of children I interviewed, particularly those who had been living in the hotels, simply disappeared. It is quite likely that they moved into temporary situations, perhaps to double-up with relatives or friends. It is also likely that many of them returned after a brief respite, as so many do, to the shelters.

Notes

Introduction

5. Though a decade . . . today. "A Status Report on Hunger and Homelessness in America's Cities: 1990," Washington, D.C.: The United States Conference of Mayors, December 1990, p. 23.

5. Homeless families . . . Wenatchee, Washington. "American Nightmare: A Decade of Homelessness in the United States," Washington, D.C.: National Coalition for the Homeless, December 1989, p. 141.

15. Poem: "In the Homeless Hotel" by Maria Pagan was published in *Women In Need News*, Vol. 2, No. 4, April 1989.

Chapter 1

17. Their parents comprise . . . homeless shelters. "A Status Report on Hunger and Homelessness in America's Cities: 1990," p. 2.

17. In New Orleans . . . homeless families. From a conversation with Jackie Harris, Director, Multiservice Center for the Homeless, New Orleans, Louisiana, July 15, 1991.

18. Among them . . . children. Jonathan Kozol, "Rachel and Her Children: Homeless Families in America," New York: Crown Publishers, Inc., 1988, p. 3.

18. One out of five . . . poverty. "Money, Income and Poverty Status in the United States, 1989," Washington, D.C.: U.S. Department of Commerce, Bureau of the Census, p. 2.

18. More poor children . . . children are poor. Terry Rosenberg, "Poverty in New York City, 1985–1988: the Crisis Continues," New York: Community Service Society of New York, 1989, p. 36.

18. The number of poor . . . going strong. Janice Molnar, Ph.D., "Home Is Where the Heart Is: The Crisis of Homeless Children and Families in New York City," New York: Bank Street College of Education, March 1988, p. 12.

18. Today . . . are poor. "Money, Income and Poverty Status in the United States, 1989," p. 10.

18. Families with a single . . . over forty percent since 1970. Molnar, *op. cit.*, p. 13.

19. At the start of 1990 . . . white children. "Money, Income and Poverty Status in the United States, 1989," p. 2.

19. A person working . . . family of four. Source: U.S. Bureau of the Census, Office of Poverty and Wealth.

20. For years, costs . . . by only 53 percent. Anna Lou Dehavenon, Ph.D., and Karen Benker, M.D., "The Tyranny of Indifference: A Study of Hunger, Homelessness, Poor Health and Family Dismemberment in 818 Households with Children in New York City in 1988–89," New York: The Action Research Project on Hunger, Homelessness and Family Health, October 11, 1989, p. 4.

21. A family of four on welfare . . . that size. From a telephone conversation with the NYC Human Resources Administration Information Line, August 8, 1991.

21. Since 1982, $6.8 billion . . . are children. Molnar, *op. cit.*, p. 12.

22. This country has known . . . extent it does today. Kim Hopper and Jill Hamberg, "The Making of America's Homeless: From Skid Row to New Poor, 1945–1984," New York: Community Service Society of New York, December 1984, p. 12.

22. Between 1978 and 1987 . . . New York City alone. Phillip Weitzman, "Worlds Apart: Housing, Race/Ethnicity and Income in New York City, 1978–1987," New York: Community Service Society of New York, 1989, p. 42.

23. But Washington . . . since 1978. Paul Leonard, Cushing Dolbeare, Ed Lazere, "A Place to Call Home: the Crisis in Housing for the Poor, National Overview," Washington, D.C.: Center on Budget and Policy Priorities, April 1989, pp. 27–28.

23. In the 1950s . . . eighteen years. New York City Housing Authority Office of Program Planning.

23. In New York . . . families. Victor Bach, "Housing: Problem Analysis and Policy Directions," New York: Community Service Society of New York, May 1986, p. 28.

26. "There were nine . . . kitchen." Jacob Riis, "How the Other Half Lives" (first published 1890), New York: Hill and Wang, 1957, p. 36.

Chapter 2

27. Many give it up . . . unaffordable for them. Rimer, *op. cit.*

28. Over 21,000 households . . . nonpayment of rent. Rimer, *ibid.*

28. More than a quarter . . . from their housing. "Report on the Legal Problems of the Homeless," New York: Association of the Bar of the City of New York, October 19, 1988, p. 35.

29. In eviction cases . . . do not. *Ibid.,* pp. 35–37.

31. Apartments are classified . . . apartments in New York City. Michael Stegman, "Housing and Vacancy Report: New York City, 1987," New York: NYC Department of Housing, Preservation and Development, April 1988, p. 124.

32. Fire destroys . . . shelters. James Dumpson, David Dinkins, "A Shelter Is Not A Home," New York: Manhattan Borough President David Dinkins Task Force on Housing for Homeless Families, March 1987, p. 32.

34. More than half . . . friends. Molnar, "Home Is Where the Heart Is," p. 20.

Chapter 3

36. Families pass . . . thousand a year. "Emergency Housing Services for Homeless Families," New York: NYC Human Resources Administration Crisis Intervention Services, September 1991, pp. 3–7.

36. In 1938 . . . public obligation." New York State Constitution, Article 17.

37. Outraged civic . . . needed it. New York State Supreme Court Cases *Callahan v. Carey, McCain v. Dinkins.* See "Litigation by the Legal Aid Society on Behalf of the Homeless in New York City," New York: Legal Aid Society Homeless Family Rights Project, July 1987, and "Cruel Brinkmanship: Planning for the Homeless — 1983," New York: Coalition for the Homeless, NY: August 16, 1982.

38. City policymakers . . . becoming homeless. Dumpson, Dinkins, "A Shelter Is Not A Home," p. 97.

38. The federal government . . . rest of the bills. The federal programs, Aid to Families with Dependent Children, and Emergency Assistance to Families, are administered by the Department of Health and Human Services.

38. In New York . . . one squalid room. "Facility List for Homeless Families," New York: NYC Human Resources Administration Crisis Intervention Services, October 1, 1989, pp. 1–5.

38. The barracks-style . . . per family. "Children In Storage: Families in New York City's Barracks-style Shelters," New York: Citizens' Committee for Children of New York, Inc., November 1988, p. 61.

41. According to . . . children in the family." 18 N.Y.C.R.R., Section 900.7A.

44. Housing experts . . . compared to the tremendous need for them. Yvonne Rafferty, Testimony for Advocates for Children of New York, Inc., before the New York City Council Committee on General Welfare, November 14, 1990.

45. Part of the reason . . . no choice. Sam Roberts, "City as Landlord:

Homeless Force Policy Turnabout," *The New York Times*, September 20, 1990, p. B1.

45. According to housing experts . . . their feet. "Housing the Homeless: A Study of the Housing and Services Provided by New York City to Homeless Families," New York: Citizens' Committee for Children of New York, Inc., 1991, p. 2.

45. Whether a family . . . the community. Lisa Glazer, "Mixed Blessings: Life After the Welfare Hotels," *City Limits* XV no. 2 (February 1990, pp. 8–13.

45. It is a sad . . . third time. James Knickman and Beth Weitzman, "A Study of Homeless Families in New York City: Risk Assessment Models and Strategies for Prevention," New York: Health Research Program of New York University, September 1989, p. 12.

Chapter 4

49. Poem: "Mixed Feelings of Being Homeless" by Vivian Natal was published in *We Are the Future,* magazine of the Saratoga Learning Center, published by The Waterways Project of Ten Penny Players, Inc., Spring 1989.

49. Health and safety problems . . . than the law permits. Steven Banks, Testimony of the Legal Aid Society Homeless Family Rights Project before the New York City Council Committee on General Welfare, April 1, 1991, p. 2.

51. Families receive a "restaurant" . . . restaurant. From a telephone conversation with the NYC Human Resources Administration Information Line, November 7, 1990.

54. The quotation from Mary is from "Shana's Day of Being a Star," in *We Are the Future,* published by The Waterways Project of Ten Penny Players, Inc., Spring 1989.

55. The quotation from Yvette is from a prepared statement by Yvette Diaz, submitted to the Select Committee on Children, Youth and Families, U.S. House of Representatives hearing on February 24, 1987.

56. Some families . . . prostitutes bring their clients. Steven Banks, testimony before the Ad Hoc Task Force on the Homeless and Housing of the Committee on the Budget, U.S. House of Representatives hearing on December 20, 1988.

59. New York City officials admit . . . but to use them. "Officials Defend Use of Welfare Hotels," *The New York Times*, September 20, 1990, p. B1.

59. Poem: "Family In Need" by Bill is from *The Get Along Gang,* magazine of the Hotel Martinique Learning Center, published by The Waterways Project of Ten Penny Players, Inc., July 1988.

Chapter 5

60. Schools, office buildings ... very limited services. "Children In Storage: Families in New York City's Barracks-style Shelters," New York: Citizens' Committee for Children of New York, Inc., November 1988, pp. 2, 27, 49.

66. As a precaution ... better their situation. *Ibid.,* p. 52.

66. All the shelters ... once during their stay. *Ibid.,* p. 49.

Chapter 6

71. Recreation, an on-site nurse ... in the neighborhood. 18 N.Y.C.R.R. Section 900.10.

71. One shelter ... permanent housing is found. From a telephone conversation with Verona Middleton-Jeter, Director, Urban Family Center of the Henry Street Settlement, February 3, 1990.

73. It is no wonder ... in welfare hotels. Andrew Cuomo, testimony before the Subcommittee on Public Assistance and Unemployment Compensation of the Ways and Means Committee, U.S. House of Representatives, and the Subcommittee on Social Security and Family Policy of the Committee on Finance, U.S. Senate, joint hearing on March 28, 1988.

74. Poem: "Homeless Saratoga" by Mike is from *Streams 3,* published by The Waterways Project of Ten Penny Players, Inc., 1989.

Chapter 7

78. Each time children ... days of school. Yvonne Rafferty, Ph.D., and Norma Rollins, "Learning in Limbo: the Educational Deprivation of Homeless Children," New York: Advocates for Children of New York, Inc., September 1989, p. 8.

81. One study found ... 57 percent citywide. *Ibid.,* p. 92.

82. Given all the obstacles ... than for others. *Ibid.,* p. 76.

Chapter 8

84. One doctor ... untreated ear infection." From a telephone conversation with Irwin Redlener, M.D., Director of the New York Childrens' Health Project, January 28, 1991, and Ilene Barth, "The Third World of Welfare Children," *New York Newsday,* January 17, 1988, p. 7.

85. But rates of underimmunization ... poor children who have homes. Garth Alperstein, M.B.Ch.B., *et al.,* "Health Problems of Homeless Children in New York City," *American Journal of Public Health* 78 no. 9, September 1988, pp. 1232–1233.

85. Parents skip meals . . . weight themselves. Anna Lou Dehavenon, Ph.D., and Karen Benker, M.D., "The Tyranny of Indifference: A Study of Hunger, Homelessness, Poor Health and Family Dismemberment in 1,325 New York City Households with Children in 1989–90," New York: The Action Research Project on Hunger, Homelessness and Family Health, October 12, 1990, p. 44.

85. Families without cooking . . . dehydration. Saundra Shepherd, M.D., Affirmation in Support of Plaintiffs, New York State Supreme Court Case *McCain v. Koch,* Index No. 41023/83, October 29, 1990.

86. Homeless preschool . . . personal/social growth. Ellen Bassuk, M.D., and Lynn Rosenberg, "Psychosocial Characteristics of Homeless Children and Children With Homes," *Pediatrics* 85 no. 3 (1990), pp. 257–261.

87. A doctor . . . pregnancy proceeds. Karen Benker, M.D., in article by Thomas Morgan, "Welfare Agency Faulted in Closing Cases," *The New York Times,* October 10, 1990, p. B3, referring to p. 45 of report by Anna Lou Dehavenon, Ph.D., and Karen Benker, M.D.

87. Not surprisingly . . . city overall. The Hon. George Miller, Chairman, Select Committee on Children, Youth and Families, U.S. House of Representatives, opening statement of hearing, February 24, 1987.

87. The infant mortality rate . . . in the city. Wendy Chavkin, *et al.,* "Reproductive Experience of Women Living in Hotels for the Homeless in New York City," *New York State Journal of Medicine,* 87, pp. 10–13.

87. One doctor . . . doctors' offices. From a telephone conversation with Dr. Irwin Redlener, Director of the New York Childrens' Health Project, New York, January 28, 1991.

88. According to one New York City . . . three and six. Edward Telzak, M.D., *et al.,* "Diarrhea in the Family Congregate Shelters of New York City," Draft #5, New York City Department of Health, 1987.

88. Outbreaks of such highly . . . shelters. Shepherd, *op. cit.*

Chapter 9

91. The quotation from Yvette is from a prepared statement by Yvette Diaz, submitted to the Select Committee on Children, Youth and Families, U.S. House of Representatives hearing on February 24, 1987.

93. Poem: "Oasis Rap" was written by children participating in Project Oasis of the Single Parent Resource Center of New York.

96. The quotation by Leon is from *The Daily Camper,* newsletter of Camp Homeward Bound (project of the Coalition for the Homeless of New York), Summer 1989, Session 3.

96. The quotation and poem by Douglas are from *The Daily Camper,* newsletter of Camp Homeward Bound (project of the Coalition for the Homeless of New York), Summer 1989, Session 3.

97. The quotation by Melanie is from *The Homeward Bound Bugle,*

newsletter of Camp Homeward Bound (project of the Coalition for the Homeless of New York), Summer 1989, Session 2.

Chapter 11

109. Poem: "Who Cares" by Sharneen is from *The Get Along Gang,* magazine of the Hotel Martinique Learning Center, published by The Waterways Project of Ten Penny Players, Inc., July 1988.

115. Poem: "The Friendship Song" by Carrie is used with her permission.

Chapter 12

128. Poem: "Somewhere Special" by Maria P. was published in *Women In Need News,* newsletter of the Women In Need residences, Jan.–Feb. 1990.

Bibliography

Alperstein, Garth, Claire Rappaport, and Joan Flanigan. "Health Problems of Homeless Children in New York City." *American Journal of Public Health* 78 no. 9 (September 1988).

"American Nightmare: A Decade of Homelessness in the United States." Washington, D.C.: National Coalition for the Homeless, December 1989.

Bach, Victor. "Housing: Problem Analysis and Policy Directions." New York: Community Service Society of New York, May 1986.

Banks, Steven, on behalf of the Legal Aid Society Homeless Family Rights Project. Testimony before the Committee on General Welfare. New York: New York City Council hearing, April 1, 1991.

————Testimony before the Ad Hoc Task Force on the Homeless and Housing, of the Committee on the Budget. Washington, D.C.: U.S. House of Representatives hearing, December 20, 1988.

Bassuk, Ellen, and Lynn Rosenberg. "Psychosocial Characteristics of Homeless Children and Children With Homes." *Pediatrics* 85 no. 3 (1990).

[Berck, Judith.] "Children In Storage: Families in New York City's Barracks-style Shelters." New York: Citizens' Committee for Children of New York, Inc., November 1988.

Chavkin, W., A. Kristal, C. Seabron, and P. E. Guigli. "Reproductive Experience of Women Living in Hotels for the Homeless in New York City," *New York State Journal of Medicine,* 87.

"Cruel Brinkmanship: Planning for the Homeless — 1983." New York: Coalition for the Homeless, August 16, 1982.

Cuomo, Andrew. Testimony before the Subcommittee on Public Assistance and Unemployment Compensation, Ways and Means Committee, and the Subcommittee on Social Security

and Family Policy, Committee on Finance. Washington, D.C.:
U.S. House of Representatives and U.S. Senate joint hearing,
March 28, 1988.

Dehavenon, Anna Lou, and Karen Benker. "The Tyranny of Indif-
ference: A Study of Hunger, Homelessness, Poor Health and
Family Dismemberment in 818 Households with Children in
New York City in 1988–89." New York: The Action Research
Project on Hunger, Homelessness and Family Health, October
11, 1989.

——————"The Tyranny of Indifference: A Study of Hunger,
Homelessness, Poor Health and Family Dismemberment in
1,325 New York City Households with Children in 1989–90."
New York: The Action Research Project on Hunger, Homelessness and Family Health, October 12, 1990.

Diaz, Yvette. Testimony before the Select Committee on Children,
Youth and Families. Washington, D.C.: U.S. House of Representatives hearing, February 24, 1987.

Dumpson, James, and David Dinkins. "A Shelter Is Not A Home."
New York: Manhattan Borough President David Dinkins Task
Force on Housing for Homeless Families, March 1987.

"Emergency Housing Services for Homeless Families." New York:
NYC Human Resources Administration Crisis Intervention
Services, June 1991.

"Facility List for Homeless Families." New York: NYC Human Resources Administration Crisis Intervention Services, October 1,
1989.

Glazer, Lisa. "Mixed Blessings: Life After the Welfare Hotels." *City
Limits* XV no. 2 (February 1990).

Hopper, Kim, and Jill Hamberg. "The Making of America's Homeless: From Skid Row to New Poor, 1945–1984." New York:
Community Service Society of New York, December 1984.

"Housing the Homeless: A Study of the Housing and Services Provided by New York City to Homeless Families." New York:
Citizens' Committee for Children of New York, Inc., 1991.

Knickman, James, and Beth Weitzman. "A Study of Homeless Families in New York City: Risk Assessment Models and Strategies
for Prevention." New York: Health Research Program of New
York University, September 1989.

Kozol, Jonathan. "Rachel and Her Children: Homeless Families in
America." New York: Crown Publishers, Inc., 1988.

Leonard, Paul, Cushing Dolbeare, and Ed Lazere. "A Place to Call
Home: the Crisis in Housing for the Poor, National Overview."
Washington, D.C.: Center on Budget and Policy Priorities, April
1989.

"Litigation by the Legal Aid Society on Behalf of the Homeless in New York City." New York: Legal Aid Society Homeless Family Rights Project, July 1987.

Miller, George. Opening statement before the Select Committee on Children, Youth and Families. Washington, D.C.: U.S. House of Representatives hearing, February 24, 1987.

Molnar, Janice. "Home Is Where the Heart Is: The Crisis of Homeless Children and Families in New York City." New York: Bank Street College of Education, March 1988.

Morgan, Thomas. "Welfare Agency Faulted in Closing Cases." *The New York Times,* October 10, 1990.

"Officials Defend Use of Welfare Hotels." *The New York Times,* September 20, 1990.

Powell, Michael. "Short on Shelters: City Admits Violating Homeless Laws." *New York Newsday,* April 2, 1991.

Rafferty, Yvonne, on behalf of Advocates for Children of New York, Inc. Testimony before the Committee on General Welfare. New York: New York City Council hearing, November 14, 1990.

Rafferty, Yvonne, and Norma Rollins. "Learning in Limbo: the Educational Deprivation of Homeless Children." New York: Advocates for Children of New York, Inc., September 1989.

"Report on the Legal Problems of the Homeless." New York: Association of the Bar of the City of New York, October 19, 1988.

[Reyes, Lilia, and Laura Waxman.] "A Status Report on Hunger and Homelessness in America's Cities: 1990." Washington, D.C.: The United States Conference of Mayors, December 1990.

Riis, Jacob. "How the Other Half Lives." New York: Hill and Wang, 1957 (first published 1890).

Rimer, Sara. "The Rent's Due, and for Many It's Homelessness Knocking." *The New York Times,* March 24, 1990.

Roberts, Sam. "City as Landlord: Homeless Force Policy Turnabout." *The New York Times,* September 20, 1990.

Rosenberg, Terry. "Poverty in New York City, 1985–1988: the Crisis Continues." New York: Community Service Society of New York, 1989.

Shepherd, Saundra. Affirmation in Support of Plaintiffs, New York State Supreme Court Case McCain *v.* Koch, October 29, 1990.

Stegman, Michael. "Housing and Vacancy Report: New York City, 1987." New York: NYC Department of Housing, Preservation and Development, April 1988.

Telzak, Edward, *et al.* "Diarrhea in the Family Congregate Shelters of New York City," Draft #5. New York: New York City Department of Health, 1987.

Weitzman, Phillip. "Worlds Apart: Housing, Race/Ethnicity and Income in New York City, 1978–1987." New York: Community Service Society of New York, 1989.

[Welniak, Edward, and Mark Littman.] "Money, Income and Poverty Status in the United States, 1989." Washington, D.C.: U.S. Department of Commerce, Bureau of the Census, September 1990.